BIBLICAL FOUNDATIONS FOR THE ECONOMIC WAY OF THINKING

A High School Homeschool Elective Course

INSTITUTE FOR
FAITH, WORK
& ECONOMICS

ISBN 978-0-9964257-7-3

Published by The Institute for Faith, Work & Economics
8400 Westpark Drive, Suite 100
McLean, Virginia 22102

www.tifwe.org

CONTENTS

COURSE INTRODUCTION

The *Biblical Foundations for the Economic Way of Thinking* course is a seventeen-week high school homeschool elective course. The course guides students through an in-depth, biblical exploration of the economic way of thinking.

Students will learn the basic principles of economics. What makes IFWE's course unique is its emphasis on learning the biblical foundations for economics as a necessary component of making God-honoring decisions.

Using a variety of readings, students will learn how thinking economically can provide a framework for living that fits God's design, brings him glory, and allows them to experience fulfillment in their lives.

When God created the world, he designed us to cultivate the flourishing of his creation and glorify him in the process. To do this, he equipped each of us with unique gifts and skills we are to use to "be fruitful and multiply and fill the earth" (Gen. 1:28). This command in Genesis is a call to stewardship. In a world of limited time and resources, we need to make good decisions in order to be faithful stewards of all God gives us.

The economic way of thinking is a tool God has given us to make decisions that fit with his design and glorify him as well as serve others.

By gaining an understanding of economics, students will learn how to make wise decisions while living under conditions of scarcity and limited knowledge. They will learn the importance of being able to freely exchange their time, abilities, and resources with others in order to produce more prosperity than they could on their own. They will gain discernment as they learn about trade-offs and opportunity costs, things that will help them make wise use of their time and create value using their unique gifts and talents.

In short, students who take this course will see how living out biblical economic principles empowers them to live faithfully as Christians, to flourish and to contribute to the flourishing of their families, their communities, their nation, and, ultimately, the world.

COURSE REQUIREMENTS

1. There is one book required for the course:

    a. Gwartney, James D., Richard L. Stroup, and Dwight R. Lee. *Common Sense Economics: What Everyone Should Know about Wealth and Prosperity.* New York: St. Martin's Press, 2005.

    b. There are also numerous readings and educational videos that can be found online.

2. A midterm and final exam will be given to help students think reflectively about the material and their own understanding of the economic way of thinking.

COURSE OBJECTIVES

After completing this course, students should:

- Understand the economic way of thinking as a path to better stewardship
- Grasp the importance of good decision making for serving God and his creation
- Understand the grounding of economic thinking in biblical principles
- Be provoked to always ask "Why?" and "At what cost?" when evaluating different economic paths

COURSE LAYOUT

Each module consists of several sections designed to guide students comprehensively through the material. Modules begin with a brief **description** of content and review of the previous material. **Learning objectives** state the main idea for the module's content. **Key ideas** highlight important concepts not to be missed in each lesson. **Scripture readings** note all Scripture references for the introductory material. **Reading assignments** list required and optional readings for related content. **Study questions** are designed to ensure reading comprehension and encourage reflection. **Assessments**, if listed, explain writing assignments designed to apply concepts presented in the material to the students' own lives. Group or family **learning activities** offer suggested group exercises to further apply and examine important concepts. A **summary** wraps up the module and prepares students for the next lesson.

SUGGESTED ANSWERS AND GRADING RUBRIC

A teacher's guide for this course, with a grading rubric, suggested answers, and guidelines, is included with the purchase of this curriculum.

CONTRIBUTORS

ANNE RATHBONE BRADLEY, PHD

Dr. Anne Rathbone Bradley is the vice president of economic initiatives at the institute, where she develops and commissions research toward a systematic biblical theology of economic freedom. She is a visiting professor at Georgetown University, and she also teaches at the Institute for World Politics and George Mason University. Additionally, she is a visiting scholar at the Bernard Center for Women, Politics, and Public Policy. Previously, she has taught at Charles University, Prague, and served as the Associate Director for the Program in Economics, Politics, and the Law at the James M. Buchanan Center at George Mason University.

She is an editor of and contributing author to IFWE's recently released book, *For the Least of These: A Biblical Answer to Poverty.* In her chapter, Dr. Rathbone Bradley examines income inequality from both an economic and biblical perspective and provides guidance to Christians on how to respond, particularly through our vocations.

Dr. Rathbone Bradley's other academic work has focused on the political economy of terrorism with specific emphasis on the industrial organization of al-Qaeda. Her research has been published in scholarly journals and edited volumes. She is currently working on a book that analyzes the political economy of al-Qaeda post–9/11. Based on her academic research, she also worked as an economic analyst for the Central Intelligence Agency's Office of Terrorism Analysis.

Dr. Rathbone Bradley received her PhD in economics from George Mason University in 2006, during which time she was a James M. Buchanan Scholar.

GREG AYERS

Greg Ayers is the senior editor at the Institute for Faith, Work & Economics, where he oversees the Institute's product creation and provides direction and support for its content development, editing, and publishing.

Before joining the Institute, Greg worked as a director of development with the Bill of Rights Institute in Arlington, VA, where he managed the institute's donor communications and direct mail and e-mail fundraising programs. He has also worked as a freelance direct mail copywriter and music journalist. He served as a fellow in the Falls Church Fellowship Program, a postgraduate leadership development program at the Falls Church Anglican in Falls Church, VA.

Greg graduated from Wheaton College in Wheaton, IL, with his bachelor in arts in political science. He resides in Arlington, VA.

ABOUT THE INSTITUTE FOR FAITH, WORK & ECONOMICS

The Institute for Faith, Work & Economics™ (IFWE) is a nonprofit, 501(c)(3) Christian research organization committed to promoting biblical and economic principles that help individuals find fulfillment in their work and contribute to a free and flourishing society.

IFWE's research starts with the belief that the Bible, as the inerrant Word of God, provides the authoritative and intellectual foundation for a proper understanding of work and economic truths that, when properly followed, can help individuals, companies, communities, and nations flourish.

IFWE's research is based on three core principles:

1. Each person is created in God's image and, like him, has a desire to be creative and to find **fulfillment** using their God-given talents through work.

2. All work, whether paid or volunteer, matters to God, and we as Christians are called to pursue excellence throughout the week—not just on Sundays—stewarding all that we've been given for God's glory and for the **flourishing** of society.

3. Therefore, we as citizens must promote an economic environment that not only provides us the **freedom** to pursue our callings and flourish in our work but also reflects the inherent dignity of every human being.

Our desire is to help Christians view their work within the bigger picture of what God is doing in the world. Not only do we help Christians find personal fulfillment, but we also help them understand how to better alleviate poverty, address greed, and view possessions properly. With a biblical view of work and economics, we can partner together to be meaningful participants in God's plan to restore the world to the way he intended it to be.

We invite you to learn more through our other resources at https://tifwe.org:

- Our blog provides brief but powerful insights.
- Our book *How Then Should We Work?* is a perfect starting point for understanding the biblical meaning of work.
- Our research offers concise explanations of our most significant research and findings.
- Sign up for our newsletter and receive updates on our latest events and publications.

SYLLABUS

The links to reading assignments that can be found online are available at: http://homeschool.tifwe.org. However, if you are accessing this book on a computer, you can access them by clicking the readings' links.

MODULE 1—GOD'S DESIGN AND DESIRE: THE PURPOSE OF ECONOMICS

1. Genesis 1–4
2. Brian Baugus, "Can Genesis Teach Us Anything about Economics?"
3. Art Lindsley, "The Call to Creativity"
4. Jonathan Pennington, "A Biblical Theology of Human Flourishing"
5. Hugh Whelchel, "Four Principles of Biblical Stewardship"
6. Hugh Whelchel, "Carrying Out the Cultural Mandate Is Essential for Biblical Flourishing"
7. Shawn Ritenour, "An Unexpected Source of Human Flourishing"
8. Econ Free, "Economic Freedom and the Quality of Life" (video)
9. IFWE, "Freedom to Flourish" (video)

MODULE 2—SELF-INTEREST AND GOD-HONORING DECISIONS

1. Art Lindsley, "C. S. Lewis, Greed, and Self-Interest"
2. Samuel Gregg, "Self Interest, Rightly Understood"
3. Anne Bradley, "Goldman Sachs, Self-Interest, and Greed"
4. Hugh Whelchel, "What Is Biblical Self-Interest?"
5. Jay W. Richards, "Selfishness, Self-Interest, and Significance"
6. Aeon J. Skoble, "Libertarian Philosophy: Why Thieves Hate Free Markets" (video)
7. Milton Friedman, "Greed" (video)

MODULE 3—THE FOUNDATIONAL IDEAS OF ECONOMICS

1. James D. Gwartney, Richard L. Stroup, and Dwight R. Lee, *Common Sense Economics*, Part 1

2. Leonard E. Read, "I, Pencil"

3. Anne R. Bradley, "You Can Spend Six Months and $1,500 Making a Chicken Sandwhich…but Should You?"

4. Adam Smith, *The Wealth of Nations*, Book 1, Chapters 1–4

5. Donald J. Boudreaux, "Comparative Advantage"

6. Russell Roberts, "Incentives Matter"

7. Steven Horwitz, "Economists and Scarcity: The Concepts of 'Scarcity' and 'Resources' Are Often Misunderstood"

8. IFWE, "I, Smartphone" (video)

9. Tyler Cowen, "Introduction to Microeconomics" (video)

MODULE 4—THE ROLE OF TRADE IN HUMAN FLOURISHING

1. Russell Roberts, "Treasure Island: The Power of Trade, Part I: The Seemingly Simple Story of Comparative Advantage"

2. Russell Roberts, "Treasure Island: The Power of Trade, Part II: How Trade Transforms Our Standard of Living"

3. R. Mark Isaac, "Does the Bible Condemn Trade?"

4. David R. Henderson, "Opportunity Cost"

5. David R. Henderson, "TANSTAAFL, There Ain't No Such Thing as a Free Lunch"

6. Hugh Whelchel, "What Are the Economic Implications of the Fall?"

7. Art Carden, "Trade Is Made of Win, Part 1: Wealth Creation" (video)

8. Thomas Sowell, "There are No Solutions, Only Tradeoffs" (video)

MODULE 5—DECENTRALIZED KNOWLEDGE, PROPERTY RIGHTS, AND PRICES

1. Friedrich August von Hayek, "The Use of Knowledge in Society"

2. Art Lindsley, "Private Property"

3. Walter Kaiser, "Ownership and Property in the Old Testament Economy"

4. Russell Roberts, "Where Do Prices Come From?"

5. Donald J. Boudreaux, "Information and Prices"

6. Shawn Ritenour, "Three Reasons Private Property Is Essential for Human Flourishing"

MODULE 6—THE MARKET PROCESS, SUBJECTIVE VALUE, AND UNPLANNED ORDER

1. Max Borders, "Subjective Value"

2. Brian Baugus, "How Does the Market Work?"

3. Russell Roberts, "The Reality of Markets"

4. Anne Bradley, "The Market Process and the Path to Flourishing"

5. Russell Roberts, "A Marvel of Cooperation: How Order Emerges without a Conscious Planner"

6. Friedrich August von Hayek, "Kinds of Order in Society"

7. Anne Bradley, "Is the Economy a Pie?"

8. Hans Rosling, "200 Countries, 200 Years, 4 Minutes" (video)

9. Tom J. Bell, "Can Order Be Unplanned?" (video)

10. Donald J. Boudreaux, "Subjective Value" (video)

11. Steven Horwitz, "Spontaneous Order and the Market Process" (video)

MODULE 7—PRICES, PROPERTY RIGHTS, AND PROFITS

1. David R. Henderson, "Demand"

2. Robert Sirico, "Why Profits are Not Exploitative"

3. Armen A. Alchien, "Property Rights"

4. Robert Sirico, "Prices Keep Profits Fair"

5. Anne Bradley, "Making a Profit: An Unexpected Way to Help Others"

6. Michael Munger, "They Clapped: Can Price-Gouging Laws Prohibit Scarcity?"

7. Alex Tabarrok, "The Demand Curve" (video)

8. Alex Tabarrok, "The Supply Curve" (video)

9. Alex Tabarrok, "The Equilibrium Price" (video)

10. Tyler Cowen, "A Deeper Look at the Demand Curve" (video)

11. Tyler Cowen, "The Demand Curve Shifts" (video)

12. Alex Tabarrok, "A Deeper Look at the Supply Curve" (video)

13. Marginal Revolution University, "The Supply Curve Shifts" (video)

14. Alex Tabarrok, "Exploring Equilibrium" (video)

MODULE 8—ECONOMIC FREEDOM AND STEWARDSHIP

1. James D. Gwartney, Richard L. Stroup, and Dwight R. Lee, *Common Sense Economics*, Parts 2 and 3

2. Alan S. Blinder, "Free Trade"

3. Anne Bradley and Joseph Connors, "Economic Freedom and the Path to Flourishing"

4. Anne Bradley, "Five Reasons Christians Should Embrace Economic Freedom"

5. Econ Free, "Episode One: Economic Freedom and Quality of Life" (video)

6. Econ Free, "Episode Two: Economic Freedom in America Today" (video)

MODULE 9—ENTREPRENEURSHIP AND INNOVATION

1. Ludwig von Mises, "Profit and Loss"

2. Wolfgang Kasper, "Competition"

3. Brian Baugus, "Entrepreneurship within a Biblical Worldview"

4. Elise Daniel, "Meet the Generation Bringing Back Entrepreneurship in America"

MODULE 10—MIDTERM

MODULE 11—ECONOMIC FREEDOM AND THE DEVELOPING WORLD

1. Sara Corbett, "Can the Cell Phone Help End Global Poverty?"

2. Laurence Chandy and Geoffrey Gertz, "With Little Notice, Globalization Reduced Poverty"

3. Robert E. Lucas Jr., "The Industrial Revolution: Past and Future"

4. Derek Thompson, "The Economic History of the Last 2,000 Years: Part II"

5. Tolu Ogunlesi and Stephanie Busari, "Seven Ways Mobile Phones Have Changed Lives in Africa"

6. The World Bank, "Mobile Phone Access Reaches Three Quarters of the Planet's Population"

7. Hans Rosling, "200 Years, 200 Countries, 4 Minutes" (video)

8. Hans Rosling, "Hans Rosling and the Magic Washing Machine" (video)

9. Donald J. Boudreaux, "The Hockey Stick of Human Prosperity" (video)

MODULE 12—THE ROOTS OF POVERTY

1. Jonathan Pennington, "'Sell Your Possessions and Give to the Poor': A Theological Reflection on Jesus' Teaching Regarding Personal Wealth and Charity"

2. Theology of Work Project, "God's Law Calls People of Means to Provide Economic Opportunities for the Poor"

3. Glenn Sunshine, "Who are the Rich and the Poor?"

4. Art Lindsley, "Five Myths about Jubilee"

5. Theology of Work Project, "Productive Opportunities for the Poor"

MODULE 13—THE ROLE OF ECONOMIC FREEDOM IN ALLEVIATING POVERTY

1. Kristine Zambito, "When It Comes to Alleviating Poverty, Here's How Your Church Can Avoid Help that Hurts"

2. Steven Horwitz, "Contemporary Economic Myths"

3. Elise Daniel, "Economic Freedom is Not Enough for Human Flourishing"

4. Robert A. Lawson, "Economic Freedom"

5. Anne Bradley, "Freedom and Flourishing"

6. Jeffrey Dorfman, "Free Markets Unquestionably Help the Poor"

7. IFWE, "Flourishing" (video)

MODULE 14—GOVERNMENT AND THE ECONOMY

1. J. P. Moreland, "A Biblical Case for Limited Government"

2. Robert P. Murphy, "The Costs of Government"

3. Donald J. Boudreaux, "Free Trade and Globalization: More than Just 'Stuff'"

4. Robert Higgs, "Government Growth"

5. James Madison, "Federalist #10"

MODULE 15—GOVERNMENT AND UNINTENDED CONSEQUENCES

1. Frédéric Bastiat, *The Law*
2. Frédéric Bastiat, "What Is Seen and What Is Not Seen"
3. Anne Bradley, "Does the Minimum Wage Hurt the People It's Trying to Help?"
4. Brian Griffiths, "Christianity, Socialism, and Wealth Creation"
5. Antony Davies, "Unintended Consequences of Price Controls" (video)
6. Alex Tabarrok, "Price Ceilings" (video)
7. Alex Tabarrok, "Price Ceilings: Rent Controls" (video)
8. Alex Tabarrok, "Price Floors: The Minimum Wage" (video)
9. Alex Tabarrok, "Price Floors: Airline Fares" (video)

MODULE 16—FINAL REFLECTIONS

1. Peter J. Boettke, *The Battle of Ideas: Economics and the Struggle for a Better World*
2. Art Lindsley, "The Biblical View of Freedom"
3. EconStories, "'Fear the Boom and the Bust' Hayek vs. Keynes Rap Anthem" (video)

MODULE 17—FINAL EXAM

MODULE 1

GOD'S DESIGN AND DESIRE: THE PURPOSE OF ECONOMICS

DESCRIPTION

This module will help you understand how economics is part of God's created order and not the "dismal science" it's known to be. God's .design for his creation is for it to glorify him and flourish. We are called to work and exercise creativity, and when we do these things and make God-pleasing decisions, he is glorified and we are able to bring about greater flourishing in creation. In this process, economics helps us become better decision makers.

LEARNING OBJECTIVES

"Learning Objectives" will briefly summarize the main points of the module. Consider the learning objectives your key takeaways for the material. You should feel confident explaining these objectives by the end of your study.

- God created us to work. While the Fall made our work and our jobs harder, this purpose still remains.

- We are created uniquely to make purposeful contributions to God's creation as his subcreators.

- When we use our gifts wisely and make good decisions, we better fulfill God's design (who we are in Christ) and his desire (what he created us to accomplish).

- Economic thinking results in good decision making, which is good stewardship, which glorifies God.

- Increased human flourishing brings glory to God and helps fulfill his desires.

KEY IDEAS

In each module, this section will briefly explain key ideas and vocabulary from the material that we don't want you to miss. These ideas and vocabulary will help you grasp each module's content. Keep in mind that some definitions are contextualized for the material of this course.

1. God's purpose for human beings:
   a. God placed us on this earth to fulfill the cultural mandate and strive toward using our scarce resources to create flourishing.
2. Human anthropology according to the Bible:
   a. Each person is created uniquely: God gave us all gifts and talents that are specific to us as individuals.
   b. Human beings are rational: We have the ability to think logically and analytically. At the same time, our knowledge and capacity to learn is finite and imperfect, like the rest of creation.
   c. Human beings were created to be purposeful: We each have a unique calling to live our lives in pursuit of the furtherance of God's kingdom.
   d. Human beings were created with self-interest: We are concerned for our personal well-being. We make choices based on our unique preferences.
   e. Human beings were created to be subcreators: We are called to subdue the slice of creation that God has entrusted to us by putting to work our gifts and talents.

INTRODUCTION

As evangelical Christians, Scripture is our guide for faith and practice in all areas of life. It is the inspired word of God, and as such, it is inerrant and applies to every aspect of our lives. It can and should inform who we are, what we were created to do, and the personal and corporate goals of our lives. We can better understand these things by looking at Genesis. The truths found in Genesis are the starting point for this study in economics.

God did not give us the Garden of Eden without the tools to "work it and take care of it" (Gen. 2:15). An important distinction needs to be made here: taking care of something means preserving it, and making sure it doesn't get destroyed. Working something, on the other hand, implies cultivating it into something more. We are to do both. The question is, how are we to do these things? The first step is to figure out who God created us to be and then to understand the principles that will make us better stewards or cultivators. Next, understanding economics is essential for our task, because at its core, economics is about the stewardship of all our resources, time, and talents.

So who has God created you to be? If you and your family have not taken IFWE's *Calling* course, we highly recommend it. The course thoughtfully explores the biblical meaning of calling to help students understand how they were created and who God is calling them to be.

Once we understand who we were created to be and for what purpose, economics helps us become the best decision makers we can be in a fallen and finite world. The term *economics* comes from the Greek word *oikonomia*, meaning "to manage a household." It is about stewarding all of our life decisions while living in a world of scarcity. We don't have to make choices and we don't bear costs when scarcity does not exist. However, in a world where time is our most limited resource, economics helps us to better steward our resources, time, and talents for God's glory.

When we become who God created us to be, we help fulfill his original desires for his creation: his glory. We can only do this when we understand both his design of creation and our unique role in it. Economics helps us to be better decision makers in a fallen world where we experience scarcity and sin.

When we embrace God's design for our lives, we are better able to use our skills to cultivate his creation for his purposes. Through the concept and practice of trade, economics helps us understand that we cannot do these things alone. Trade allows us to serve each other. It allows us to collaborate with anonymous strangers and serve hundreds, if not thousands, of people.

We play an important role in God's larger story when we do our jobs well, whether as accountants, small business owners, or large hedge fund managers. Regardless of your vocation, you can bring God glory when you do your job with excellence. You also have powerful incentives to serve others.

In this module, we start in Genesis to see that we are made uniquely and not self-sufficient. The differences between individuals make it necessary for us to come together through trade to serve each other. Good economics starts with biblical anthropology, or the study of who we are as humans and the purpose we're meant to serve. Who are we in Christ, and what we are meant to accomplish while on Earth?

ASSIGNMENTS

All articles are available online at http://homeschool.tifwe.org. This section will list required and optional reading assignments for each module.

1. Genesis 1–4
2. Brian Baugus, "Can Genesis Teach Us Anything about Economics?"

3. Art Lindsley, "The Call to Creativity"

4. Jonathan Pennington, "A Biblical Theology of Human Flourishing"

5. Hugh Whelchel, "Four Principles of Biblical Stewardship"

6. Hugh Whelchel, "Carrying Out the Cultural Mandate Is Essential for Biblical Flourishing"

7. Shawn Ritenour, "An Unexpected Source of Human Flourishing"

8. Econ Free, "Economic Freedom and the Quality of Life" (video)

9. IFWE, "Freedom to Flourish" (video)

STUDY QUESTIONS

In a few sentences, answer each of the questions below after completing the assigned reading.

1. When does trade and potential for trade occur in Genesis? Are we created to serve each other through our gifts?

2. Can we flourish alone? Why or why not?

3. How does human nature make us interdependent?

4. How can we live out the cultural mandate in different forms?

5. How does our God-given creativity help us bring about flourishing?

6. Can accountants, engineers, and others in "secular" occupations bring glory to God?

7. What is the distinction between biblical flourishing and typical cultural definitions of flourishing?

GROUP OR FAMILY ACTIVITY

This section includes optional learning activities that promote discussion, personal reflection, and sharing among your family or group. The activities are suggestions, but feel free to adapt them to your group or come up with your own.

1. Have each family or group member write on an index card what they think God has called them to be. On the back of each card, ask each member to write down three things they like doing and think they do well.

2. Talk about each person's card. Do the items on the front of the cards match the skills on the back? What can each person learn from this?

SUMMARY

Economics is a set of tools that helps us look clearly at the true costs and expected benefits of our choices. It starts with the premise of self-interest, which is precisely how God made us. The fall of humankind into sin tainted our desires and made it impossible to center them on Christ. Sin entered the world and made everything harder, including our work. Salvation in Christ gives us the ability to serve him by centering our desires on him, although imperfectly. We need the economic way of thinking to help us make better, wiser choices in a world of scarcity, imperfect knowledge, and sin. Economics helps us to look beyond short-term circumstances to the potential long-term and unintended consequences of our actions.

We are responsible for bringing about biblical flourishing. Material well-being is a part of that, as Dr. Jonathan Pennington argues.[1] God does not want us to live in poverty, struggling daily to find our next meal or dying early from a lack of medical care. Economics is a tool for bringing about biblical flourishing. It helps us to better order our personal lives by helping us focus on our comparative advantages. It helps us to see trade as a fantastic way to use our gifts to serve others across the globe as we seek to bring about more community and global flourishing.

What we will begin to explore in the next few modules are the core questions economists are always forced to ask: "Why?", "At what cost?", and "What are the alternatives?" When we see problems in the world, we need to analyze why they happen and what incentives people are responding to. We always need to assess costs against benefits—how much is it worth to proceed down a given path, and what are the alternative options available to us?

---

1. Jonathan Pennington, "A Biblical Theology of Human Flourishing," Institute for Faith, Work & Economics, March 4, 2015, http://tifwe.org/resource/a-biblical-theology-of-human-flourishing-2/.

MODULE 2

SELF-INTEREST AND GOD-HONORING DECISIONS

DESCRIPTION

Self-interest is part of how God designed us. As his sub-creators, he made us to always be improving and innovating. When we pursue our self-interest in a biblical manner within the framework of good decisions that glorify God, we bring about greater levels of flourishing. When we pursue our self-interest by putting ourselves ahead of Christ, we bring about curses, and God's desires are not fulfilled. Self-interest is the biblical mechanism of human choice. It is motivated by our subjective value; what we want and desire, which must be Christ-centered in order for us to contribute to and experience greater flourishing.

LEARNING OBJECTIVES

Self-interest is tied to the theme of subjective value and God's design and desires that we have thus far developed.

We have a framework for making decisions:

1. The decision making mechanism involves two parts: 1.) the process we use to make a decision, and 2.) the judgment in terms of virtue (did we make a good decision?).

2. The mechanism we use to make a decision is always the same and we all have it. We always consider the circumstances and the alternatives, and choose what seems best at the time.

3. God designed us to make decisions (process), and he desires for us to make God-pleasing decisions (quality).

4. *Subjective value* is how we determine what is best when making our decisions. It is based on our preferences and, as such, is highly personal. We are always trying to improve our conditions and our own levels of happiness

5. Self-interest

   a. Central to how we make decisions; we are motivated to do what is in our best interest, to improve our conditions.

   b. Selfishness is putting yourself first, always. Refer to Philippians 2 ("Don't only consider yourself").

6. Once we are saved, the way we think about what's best for ourselves is renewed, although it's still imperfect. Now we have the ability to make decisions that are pleasing to God.

7. When we are saved, the way we determine what is "good" changes. We desire to please God, and that impacts the decisions we make. However, we still use the same decision-making process.

   a. God's common grace allows increased flourishing in the world from good decisions made by non-believers. He uses his power to suppress evil so that humankind is never as evil as they could be. He chooses, by his grace, to use nonbelieving people to do good things for his creation.

KEY IDEA

1. Self-interest is part of our design in God. Greed is the result of our own sinful desires. Greed and self-interest are not synonymous. Because of humankind's fallen nature, all people can be affected by greed—an overwhelming and often selfish hunger for something. Greedy people will stop at nothing when trying to satisfy their desires—they may even act in ways that are harmful to themselves. Self-interest also affects all people, but it is not a consequence of the Fall. Rather, self-interest drives people to take care of themselves by performing activities that range from preparing a meal or investing their money in a new venture. This pursuit of increasing personal well-being often benefits others in the process.

INTRODUCTION

Last week, we learned in Genesis about our mandate from God to use our skills for bringing about greater levels of flourishing in this fallen world of scarcity. This week, we will explain how this works through individual choice by discussing our God-given design and how those characteristics can lead to flourishing in an economy of trade which relies on self-interest.

When people have the opportunity to trade, value is created because everyone perceives value subjectively and we value different things and at different rates. We are motivated to trade with each other because of this. Through trade, individuals mutually benefit when they exchange things they value less for things they value more.

Let's go one step further. What underlies the subjective value we place on things? When we think about instances in which both parties chose to trade, self-interest was at play.

The economy, a manifestation of all trading that is constantly occurring amongst individuals, guides us to human flourishing, for God gave us the system to bring about flourishing based on our human nature. We were created as individuals with different preferences and the ability to apply subjective value. Trade allows us to create value as we continue to trade for what we value more than what we currently own and we will learn more about that next week. This idea of only trading when we value something more than what we possess leads us to the idea that the economy is driven by self-interest. In an economy of mutually beneficial trades, this self-interest is inextricably linked to making others better off. When every person is able to live out their choices, the market directs self-interest to make people better off than they otherwise would be. While the market cannot cure a greedy heart, it can encourage people to not act upon every greedy impulse.

It is important to understand self-interest as the Bible portrays it. Self-interest is part of our anthropology. It is important to keep in mind that *self-interest is not the same as selfishness*. Scripture tells us in Philippians 2:4 that it is acceptable to pursue our self-interest, but that we must still consider the interests of other people: "Let each of you look not only to his own interests, but also to the interests of others."

Self-interest is what drives people to take care of themselves, meet their needs, and pursue their subjective value. It is entirely biblical, as we are put on this earth to live life to the fullest, not to merely exist without the inclination for improvement. In an economy of trade, one's well-being increases only if it benefits others in the process.

Consider an entrepreneur who wants to provide a new product. He or she is driven to make a profit, because profit will enable him or her to sustain and grow their business. In a market economy, the entrepreneur's self-interest results in a profit only if he or she provides something that makes other peoples' lives better. In this case, self-interest drives the entrepreneur to innovate and respond to a need in society, because he or she will only make a profit by meeting others' needs first.

ASSIGNMENTS

1. Art Lindsley, "C. S. Lewis, Greed, and Self-Interest"
2. Samuel Gregg, "Self Interest, Rightly Understood"
3. Anne Bradley, "Goldman Sachs, Self-Interest, and Greed"
4. Hugh Whelchel, "What Is Biblical Self-Interest?"

5. Jay W. Richards, "Selfishness, Self-Interest, and Significance"

6. Aeon J. Skoble, "Social Cooperation: Why Thieves Hate Free Markets" (video)

7. Milton Friedman, "Greed" (video)

OPTIONAL RESOURCES

- Wesley Gant, "Greed Is Not Good (But Self-Interest Is)"
- James L. Doti, "Capitalism and Greed"

STUDY QUESTIONS

In a few sentences, answer each of the questions below after completing the assigned reading.

1. How do you act on your self-interest in your daily life?

2. What are the ways that this, for you, could turn into greed?

3. Are rich people necessarily greedy? Why or why not?

4. How does economics help us understand how self-interest can be used to serve others?

GROUP OR FAMILY ACTIVITY

Parent/teacher: Have a conversation about what the students want to be when they grow up. Ask the student why they want to provide that good or service in the economy, and consider which reasons can be labeled "self-interest" (e.g., they enjoy the particular field, they want to provide for their future family, they want to leave a certain legacy behind). Then, consider everything that would make them good at fulfilling that role and pinpoint how they are also subject to the other party's self-interest if they want to succeed.

SUMMARY

Self-interest is biblical and inherent to the way the market economy directs flourishing. When people have choices in an economy of scarce time and resources, it is in one's self-interest to make others' lives better off since such an economy is made up of mutually beneficial exchanges. When everyone has the choice to supply or consume in the market, one cannot become better off unless they provide something that someone else needs. As the voluntary and mutually beneficial exchanges compound, we work toward flourishing.

It is important to distinguish between self-interest, selfishness, and greed. Self-interest is part of our God-given anthropology and functions for the good of all when we trade our gifts and talents in the market. Selfishness and greed, on the other hand, are the results of a sinful heart. The market can correct for greed, or the greedy can use the market to their advantage. In the second case, this is not the fault of the market, but the fault of a sinful heart. While the greedy profiteer may be sinful, he only profits if other people benefit. This does not excuse the sin of greed, but it does insulate the market participants who are not greedy from being harmed. Again, we see how economics helps us to be better stewards. As self-interested individuals, the economy brings us together to make the best of our God-given anthropology. It is in your self-interest to provide something that someone else values, whether at your desk job, your small business, or as the CEO of a Fortune 500 company. Both parties are self-interested, and value creation results as you provide a good or service that the other party accepts.

Next week we will further explain how an economy of trade overcomes other limitations of our human anthropology and this fallen world. As humans, we experience a knowledge problem. We cannot know everything about everything all the time. Fortunately, God has given us the market system as a way to communicate knowledge that our minds cannot fully encompass.

MODULE 3

THE FOUNDATIONAL IDEAS OF ECONOMICS

DESCRIPTION

The economic way of thinking helps us to understand that we are a part of a much bigger story and that none of our work occurs in a vacuum. Let's say your summer job is working at a store. You may be asked to clean the floors and refill the paper towels. These jobs aren't there just for you to earn a paycheck. The store owner pays you to do these things because it's cheaper for you to do it than for him or her to do it. Our work is interconnected with the work of others, and it is incumbent upon us to figure out who God made us to be so that we can do our work well and serve as many people as possible. These ideas are known as comparative advantage and specialization, and they are the cornerstone of trading activity. All of this rests upon making good decisions within the framework of God's design and desires for us, and knowing that when we do even the smallest jobs well, we contribute to our own flourishing and the flourishing of others.

LEARNING OBJECTIVES

- Comparative advantage is an economics term that describes who we are as humans: low-cost providers of a few things and high-cost providers of many things, relative to others. Comparative means that this advantage is always relative and must be evaluated based on our trading group (the people dividing up the work that needs to be done).

- When we can come together and trade we can hone in on our comparative advantages. Working in our comparative advantage prevents us from having to do many things we aren't so good at doing.

- As people created in the image of God, we are purposeful. As such, we make decisions based on the perceived incentives we face. Market economies give us incentives (through prices, profits and losses, and property rights) to cultivate our gifts, serve others, and be entrepreneurial.

KEY IDEAS

1. Economics comes from Genesis and the Garden of Eden.

   a. The ideas of creation, work, and stewardship are inseparable from the story told in Genesis about creation and the cultural mandate God gave to Adam and Eve to care for the Garden of Eden. Economics is a tool to help us make the best uses of our resources in a world of scarcity. It helps us create new and better things. It enables us to better work with and steward the resources, time, and talents God has given us.

2. Economics makes the best of human anthropology to direct us toward flourishing.

   a. Economics is driven by our human design. Economic thinking enables us to be better off than we would be otherwise. The idea of comparative advantage parallels our uniqueness as individuals with different gifts and talents who are called to be sub-creators. Market forces help our limited rational faculties and use our self-interest to allocate resources better than our imperfect knowledge can allow.

INTRODUCTION

This week we will begin exploring the foundational ideas and principles of economics. These ideas come straight from Scripture. While the Bible is not an economics textbook where you can find words like "comparative advantage," we can tie principles of economics to the job description God has laid out for us in the cultural mandate. Biblical stewardship is the tool we use to bring about flourishing, and it requires us to find ways to organize and manage our scarce resources to comply with and advance biblical principles. The economic way of thinking does just that. It helps us understand that we can bring about greater levels of flourishing for Christians and non-Christians alike on a global scale. One does not have to be a Christian for the biblical principles found in good economic thinking to work.

For example, as we learned in the previous module, we are made in the image of God and are self-interested creatures. This can work for our good and the good of others, too. When we work to be Christ-centered and let him guide our desires, we find greater joy and fulfillment, and our desires are in line with what he seeks for us. Sin damages and complicates our desires. As a result, and because we live in a fallen world, sometimes our otherwise good self-interest becomes corrupt, turning into greed, sinful desires, or the destruction and harm of others for our own gain. This is why we need systems that direct our self-interest for the good of others. How can this happen? It happens when we are incentivized to serve others and make prudent, often sacrificial, uses of our resources. Why would an entrepreneur reinvest all of his or her earnings into the company instead of consuming them? The long-term pursuit of profit encourages this reinvestment by the entrepreneur, one person, but the byproduct is what matters—more options and alternatives for more people over the long run. This is the essence of material well-being.

In this module, you will read Deuteronomy 30:6–20, which is a fantastic example of what God desires for us on earth. It is one of the most concise and specific articulations of how God wants us to work. As sojourners in a land that is not what we have been promised, we can see that the economy is the same for us. God has changed our hearts so that we will love him, but not perfectly. If we obey his commands and statutes, all he has decreed and revealed to us, he will bless the work of our hands and there will be flourishing (Deut. 30:16). If we disobey or do things contrary to his ways, we will be cursed and there will be suffering (Deut. 30:19; Prov. 13:15: "the way of a transgressor is hard," KJV). We cannot do this perfectly, of course, but God calls us to make God-pleasing decisions (2 Cor. 5:9). When we make God-honoring decisions, we will experience greater blessings than when we choose to ignore God within our personal decision-making framework.

Subjective value, as we'll see in the next module, is an important concept in economics. When we choose to make God-honoring, Christ-centered decisions, our subjective value (that is, what we choose and what we prefer, whatever drives our desires) changes. There are many factors, including our unique dispositions resulting from how God uniquely crafted each one of us. It also includes the desire to know God and obey him, and the desire to flee from sin. Setting our eyes on God and pursuing his will leads to greater flourishing because it frees us to focus on our comparative advantage. This is liberating.

The realities of economic thinking are nonnegotiable. They are part of God's created order, and when we respect them (in the same way we respect the laws of physics), we experience more personal fulfillment and societal flourishing. When we operate in ignorance of these laws, life is harder for everyone.

ASSIGNMENTS

1. James D. Gwartney, Richard L. Stroup, and Dwight R. Lee, *Common Sense Economics, Part 1*

2. Leonard E. Read, "I, Pencil"

3. Anne R. Bradley, "You Can Spend Six Months and $1,500 Making a Chicken Sandwich…but Should You?"

4. Adam Smith, *The Wealth of Nations*, Book 1, Chapters 1–4

5. Donald J. Boudreaux, "Comparative Advantage"

6. Russell Roberts, "Incentives Matter"

7. Steven Horwitz, "Economists and Scarcity: The Concepts of 'Scarcity' and 'Resources' Are Often Misunderstood"

8. IFWE, "I, Smartphone" (video)

9. Tyler Cowen, "Introduction to Micro Economics" (video)

OPTIONAL RESOURCES

- Peter J. Boettke, "Austrian School of Economics"
- Stephen R. C. Hicks, "Ethics and Economics"
- Russell Roberts, "Charity"

STUDY QUESTIONS

In a few sentences, answer each of the questions below after completing the assigned reading.

1. How can we think about biblical stewardship in the context of economics?
2. Why do we need incentives to make decisions? Can't we just rely on altruism?
3. How and why does division of labor make sense biblically and economically? What are the advantages of division of labor for the individual, as well as for society?
4. Does anyone know how to make a pencil? Why does this matter?
5. What does market trade do? On what does it rely?
6. What is subjective value, and how is it part of God's created design? How does it affect our choices? What can change our subjective values?

GROUP OR FAMILY ACTIVITY

1. Watch the movie *Castaway*. (Note to parents: This movie is rated PG-13.)
2. Parents or group leaders: have your children track all the things they do in the morning from when they wake up to when they are ready to leave for school. What did they do? What products did they use? What did they eat? Did they get into a vehicle, or use a computer? How many things do we rely on each day that we have no idea how to make? Because we can rely on strangers to create these things, we are liberated to do things we are relatively better at doing. Have your children bring their findings to the dinner table and discuss them. How many strangers do they think were involved in making these products possible?

SUMMARY

This week, we started learning some of the principle topics in economics: comparative advantage, subjective value, the importance of incentives, self-interest, and scarcity. We will continue building an understanding of why our interdependence requires a system to bring us together to trade. We will also see how trade makes it possible for us to focus on doing the things we do better relative to anyone else, while freeing us from having to do things we're bad at. This will always change as our trading partners and technologies change.

Comparative advantage is one of the most important and perhaps misunderstood concepts in economics. It helps us realize we were not created to do all things well, and that trade allows us to conquer some of our scarcity by fostering specialization and the division of labor.

Adam Smith had these profound insights over two hundred years ago, and it is easy to see that they come straight from scripture. We are uniquely made in God's image to use our creativity to advance the flourishing of his creation. More importantly, this allows us to see glimpses of hope, of the way things could and will be when God's creation is restored.

MODULE 4

THE ROLE OF TRADE IN HUMAN FLOURISHING

DESCRIPTION

The key lesson we learned last week is that we are limited and finite. That is why we need to be in a community and trade with others. Our God-designed nature is that we are bound and finite. We can't possibly produce everything we rely upon to thrive. Think of all the things you rely on each and every day, and how difficult it would be if you had to produce them all on your own. Not only are we limited in our gifts, but we are unique in our desires as well. This concept is known as subjective value. We each prefer different kinds of music, art, colors, and styles. These unique desires change depending on time, our circumstances, other things or needs we have, new knowledge, etc. Different people desire different things as a part of our uniqueness, which means that people will want to trade for different things to meet different desires and will often value the same thing differently.

LEARNING OBJECTIVES

- When we come together through trade we are able to focus on our own gifts and become better at what God has created us to do. If you become an accountant you are trading your gifts of accounting for money from those who don't have gifts of accounting, or are less gifted than you are. You may very well purchase a car from someone else, which alleviates you from having to make the car on your own.

- Nothing is ever free. Every choice has a cost because of the scarcity of time in which we live. Apply this concept of scarcity to all choices, as even what we trade for imposes costs upon us.

- When trade occurs between two parties (individuals or companies), it is always win-win. Both parties of the trade have come together based on their subjective preferences and value what they receive more than what they forfeit.

- Trade helps us to lower the opportunity costs of consumption.

KEY IDEAS

1. Economics helps us be good stewards and overcome (but not conquer) scarcity.

   a. Economics is ultimately about being a good steward of God's creation and our talents. Our time is our most precious resource and if we are here to fill the earth, and subdue it, we cannot waste any time or any of our talents. Economics helps us to be better decision makers on the margin by weighing the costs and benefits of our decisions and looking to the future for potential unexpected consequences of our choices. When we do this well, we can make better choices, which glorify God and bring about flourishing.

INTRODUCTION

This week we will learn more about trade and its value for increasing our choices, consumption possibilities, prosperity, and levels of flourishing. Because we are finite human beings, we cannot create everything we need. We cannot create everything we want. We need a societal mechanism that allows us to venture into trade with strangers.

How can we trust the people with whom we exchange and do business? How can we know they have virtue, that they care about the products they sell? In a fallen, sinful world we must have strong incentives to encourage us to care about the products we are selling to strangers. The market process does just that, and while it cannot do that perfectly, the process of profit and loss gives a strong sense of discipline to entrepreneurs and encourages them, more often than not, to care about the products they develop and their quality. We don't have to know everyone with whom we trade, and we seldom do. This allows us to grow our skills through specialization and the division of labor.

It's been this way since the beginning of creation. The Garden of Eden was perfect but not finished. God made the garden and all things in it, and we, as people made in his image, are the crowning jewel of his creation. We are made with a purpose: to use our gifts to cultivate the earth and bring about more flourishing. On the sixth day, God looked at his creation and proclaimed that it was "very good" because now there existed all things needed to fulfill our job as stewards. In this regard, we can say that although the smart phone did not exist in the garden, everything needed for it to be created did exist. Yet the work of innovation and creativity is one of human capital, and the discovery process of entrepreneurship, like all of creation, was harmed by the Fall. Knowledge became dispersed and tacit, making its discovery difficult and laden with human error. The cell phone is a good product of human discovery, but it took much longer to emerge because of our sin and the difficulty now associated with work after the Fall.

Trade allows us to bring about more flourishing in a fallen world than there otherwise would be. It frees us from having to figure everything out on our own. Rather, we can focus on the things we are relatively better at doing. This is one of the key insights of economics: talent and skills are relative and must be compared to those around us. This comparison then serves as our guide for how we should direct our creative energies. Our personal subjective values drive what we like in terms of art, work, entertainment, and hobbies. Economic choice and calculation helps us actualize these choices through trade with others. Trade is what economists refer to as a positive-sum game—as long as it is voluntary. When you go to the grocery store and trade some of your income for apples, it frees you from having to grow and cultivate the apples yourself. You are now free to put the time, money, talent, and energy you would have spent growing and cultivating apples toward using your gifts in the way God has created you to use them. We raise the cost of living out God's call for our lives whenever we inhibit trade. Freedom to choose how we use our resources is essential to progress and making people being better off. With no ability to trade, everyone perishes. Restrictions on freedom of choice (trade) reduce flourishing.

Trade occurs within the process of free markets, providing incentives for Christians and non-Christians alike to focus on their relative gifts, work with integrity, and serve one another. In many parts of the world, the last two hundred years have been a phenomenal lesson in what happens both locally and globally when we are free to trade: massive wealth has been accumulated and poverty is on the decline.

ASSIGNMENTS

1. Russell Roberts, "The Power of Trade, Part I: The Seemingly Simple Story of Comparative Advantage"

2. Russell Roberts, "The Power of Trade, Part II: How Trade Transforms Our Standard of Living"

3. R. Mark Isaac, "Does the Bible Condemn Trade?"

4. David R. Henderson, "Opportunity Cost"

5. David R. Henderson, "TANSTAAFL, There Ain't No Such Thing as a Free Lunch"

6. Hugh Whelchel, "What are the Economic Implications of the Fall?"

7. Art Carden, "Trade Is Made of Win, Part I: Wealth Creation" (video)

8. Thomas Sowell, "There are No Solutions, Only Tradeoffs" (video)

STUDY QUESTIONS

In a few sentences, answer each of the questions below after completing the assigned reading.

1. What does it mean to say that scarcity will always be with us? Why does this make economics important?

2. What does it mean to think like an economist?

3. Apply the economic way of thinking to the following scenarios:

   a. You are a lawyer and a mother. What would you take into consideration if you are thinking about hiring a maid?

   b. You can take an airplane or a bus from Washington, DC, to New York City. The plane takes one hour and costs $190. The bus takes four hours and costs $40. Which would you take if you were a lawyer? Which would you take if you were a waitress? Discuss all the factors that would go into your decision.

4. How does the economic way of thinking allow us to overcome the economic problem of scarcity?

5. Do mutually beneficial trades always create value, even though we have the same scarce resources? Why or why not?

6. Discuss the link between opportunity cost, comparative advantage, and scarcity.

7. Why is it important to consider opportunity cost when making a decision?

GROUP OR FAMILY ACTIVITY
THE TRADING GAME

This is a great game to play with a large group of people. Invite your friends, relatives, or church small group over and increase the fun.

After playing the game, answer these questions:

- When did trades take place?

- How was value created for each individual?

- How was value created for the entire economy?

- Why did the amount of value increase even though the items traded did not change?

- What would happen if everyone was taxed 25 percent, how would you collect the tax? (Hint: You would have to break the items and destroy some of their original use and value)

- Why didn't everyone value every item exactly the same? How does this tie back to God's creation of us?

HOW TO RUN THE TRADING GAME

Parent/Teacher: The trading game is a fantastic experience for your students. It gets them up and moving around and really allows them to see how they are much more limited alone than when they are allowed to trade goods with each other. This is a good demonstration of how we are uniquely created and gifted, but are not good at doing all things. The game teaches that despite our limitations, we can experience two things when we are allowed to increase our trading partners: more flourishing for ourselves and the ability to make greater contributions to the flourishing of others by offering them our gifts, goods, and services.

The game can be done either in a one-hour or ninety-minute class depending on the size of your class. This game can be done with as few as eight to as many as one hundred people. It requires you to come prepared with bags and instructions for the four trading rounds. Once you have completed the trading rounds, either in that class or the next class meeting you can use the experience to talk about some basic economic principles as listed below:

1. We are limited in what we can produce by ourselves.

2. We are happier (we can consume more and have more free time) when we trade.

3. Trading opens us up to benefit from the gifts and skills of others.

4. When we trade with greater numbers of people, we have greater access to goods and services.

5. Subjective value drives what we like and don't like. It motivates us to trade or abstain from trading.

6. Our self-interest is manifested in our subjective value.

7. Any time we limit trade we limit opportunities for people to use their gifts, which reduces satisfaction.

8. Everyone's happiness (satisfaction) increases when we trade, not just our own.

9. Voluntary trade is a positive-sum game (both parties benefit from the trade even without money changing hands). Each gives up something that they value less to receive something they value more, making both parties better off.

INSTRUCTIONS FOR PREPPING THE BAGS BEFORE CLASS

1. Order piñata filler and trinkets from Oriental Trading (they are very inexpensive).

2. Order colored paper bags or plain brown lunch bags and write colors on the front. You will need one bag per student.

3. Divide the bags into four groups. For example, blue, orange, green, and red.

4. Open all the bags on a table.

5. The way you fill the bags is strategic. At first only two teams will be allowed to trade (say red and green), so what is in their bags needs to be slightly different. The blue and orange team will also trade, and what is in their bags needs to be slightly different, too.

6. Fill the bags with five to seven items per bag using candy (tootsie rolls, jolly ranchers, Hershey's kisses, etc.), games, trinkets, and toys.

7. The key is to make sure that some folks get multiple of an item so you can talk about why trade is good for that person (why would someone need three Slinkys?) Also talk about diminishing marginal utility (why might the second Slinky make you less satisfied than the first?)

8. See the Excel sheet at http://homeschool.tifwe.org to show how to divide the bags.

INSTRUCTIONS FOR THE STUDENTS

- **Make students get into teams of four.** Each team is the same "color." Each student gets one bag.

- **Round 1:** Tell them not to open their bag until you say "Go!" When you say "Go," they are to open their bag and not share the contents with anyone. They are to rank their happiness (or satisfaction) level on a scale from one to ten. One is the worst, ten is the best. Give them three minutes to assess their happiness level. Get each student to shout out their level and then write on the board. Then talk about how happy each team is (total of individual scores) and how happy the entire room is.

- **Round 2:** Now the trade opens up within teams. The blue team trades with each other. They can open the bag and show each other what is in it and trade however they want. The orange team trades with each other. The red team trades with each other, and the green team trades with each other. When you say "Go!" they have five minutes to trade within their team. After five minutes get each person's happiness level and write it on the board. Talk about how it has changed and why.

- **Round 3:** The orange team trades with the blue team only. The red team trades with the green team only. Give them five minutes to trade. Record the scores on the board for each person and team.

- **Round 4:** All teams trade with each other (global free trade). Give them five minutes, and they can record their scores. The point of packing the bags with different items based on their group is that they will now see items that they have never seen before.

- **Talk about the results.** How did we each get happier? Did some people not trade? Why? Did some start consuming the candy before the trading was done (consumption vs. investment)? Why does increasing the number of trading partners matter? Why did some people want to unload items they had multiples of? Why did some like some things that others didn't like (subjective value)? There are many economic principles which can and should be drawn out here and discussed. They get to keep the bags! It is a lively event.

Here are some principles that can be pulled out of this game and discussed among the participants:

Subjective value: You want different things based on your own preferences. You might value the same things as someone else, but you don't value them equally (we might trade two Hershey's kisses for one Starburst). We also may have been given things we did not like at all and worked to get rid of them.

The value of increased trading partners: As you are able to trade with more and more people in your group, you have greater alternatives. More options mean you have greater abilitiy to increase our satisfaction. To increase your satisfaction, you must offer something someone else will accept. Trade demonstrates mutual benefit because parties will only trade if it makes them more satisfied.

Decreasing marginal utility: The more you have of one thing, the less valuable each item is. Even if you love chocolate, you get less from the hundredth piece than you do from the first. Our preferences can be satiated. This will drive how much you trade and when.

Incentives: Your subjective value and desire to increase your current levels of satisfaction motivated you to trade. If you were perfectly happy with your first bag and did not believe that your happiness could be improved, you might not have traded at all. This is a gamble, because you don't know what others have to offer.

Self-interest vs. greed: You trade based on your self-interest, which is driven by your subjective preferences (what you like). Trading based on that when others can also trade for the same reasons makes everyone better off. Greed might involve stealing, lying, cheating, or defrauding others to get what you want. This is never a win-win (or positive-sum game). Greed always involves winners and losers.

SUMMARY

All choices involve costs. In every choice there is something that we did not choose because we live in a finite world marked by scarcity. Scarcity existed even before the Fall because we have always been human and finite. Scarcity is exacerbated by the Fall, and, as Genesis tells us, even the ground is cursed because of sin. Work becomes harder, flourishing is often untenable, and our reality is unpredictable. In a world of scarcity riddled with sin, we need a system to help us not only help ourselves, but also help others find fulfillment and flourish. We must first start with the idea that there is no such thing as a free lunch. Every decision involves a cost and hence a trade-off. We must weigh these costs all the time.

This is how economics helps us to be better stewards. We learn to count costs and look at the possible unintended, unforeseen consequences of our actions. We are better able to navigate an uncertain and unpredictable world when we can more fully count the costs of our decisions. If we don't count costs, how could we ever fully understand benefits? We couldn't. Benefits must be reconciled against the costs of obtaining the desired outcome. Next week we will extend these ideas to the concept of subjective value and how we use our God-given self-interest to pursue flourishing for others and ourselves within an unpredictable world driven by scarcity.

MODULE 5

DECENTRALIZED KNOWLEDGE, PROPERTY RIGHTS, AND PRICES

DESCRIPTION

As humans we have imperfect, limited knowledge, which makes it harder to overcome our conditions of scarcity and lower our relative opportunity costs. Because we don't possess all the knowledge we need to make God-honoring decisions, we must find ways to collect, harness, and simplify knowledge. Knowledge is decentralized, local, and often "man on the street." The knowledge necessary to run or plan an economy does not exist in one place and is not available to one mind. The question of flourishing makes it imperative for us to have a system of trade that fosters the transfer of knowledge and economizes on what we need to know. Prices help us in this regard. They act as signals of changing underlying levels of scarcity, and they give us information that would be difficult or impossible for us to acquire in any other way.

LEARNING OBJECTIVES

- Knowledge is local and decentralized and never available to one mind in concentrated form.

- Humans are limited in what they can know and what they can digest, so we need systems that foster the transfer of knowledge and help synthesize sophisticated knowledge.

- Students will begin to apply knowledge constraints to prices and other economic activities.

KEY IDEAS

1. Decentralized knowledge is part of human anthropology. Even before the Fall we were limited beings, never exactly like God. The fall of humankind into sin makes acquiring knowledge more difficult. Like the rest of our faculties, our rational faculties are finite and flawed, and our existence in scarcity limits how much we can know.

2. *Property ownership* ties into incentives and aids the use of scarce resources. People who own property have an incentive to care for and improve their property because it is theirs and

they will enjoy the benefit of their actions. They only serve to benefit by stewarding what they own. If property is held in common, or if property rights are insecure, there is little or no incentive to maintain, invest, and improve property because others will (or will not) steward the property and take a share of the profit or benefit. The relationship between investment and return is not certain or guaranteed. Property rights serve as the basis for the formation of prices through trade which economizes on knowledge and lowers opportunity and transactions costs.

INTRODUCTION

This week we will further explain how trade helps us overcome other limitations of our human anthropology and the fallen nature of this world. As humans, there is only so much we can know, and some of the things we know, no one else knows. Therefore knowledge is limited and dispersed. We cannot have all dynamic knowledge of everything all the time. Fortunately, God has given us the market system as a way to communicate knowledge our minds cannot fully encompass.

Every economic agent has unique knowledge of their own preferences, and no one else can have direct access to that information. The knowledge we need to discover new ways of doing things is dispersed and difficult to obtain. Nobel laureate Friedrick A. Hayek calls this the *knowledge problem* and often refers to knowledge as "man on the spot" knowledge.[1] When he says "man on the spot," Hayek means local knowledge that is accessible only to the people in a given situation. If you're in a traffic jam, only you and your fellow drivers have the immediate knowledge of your situation. The knowledge problem characterizes human existence.

When we make choices about how to use our scarce resources, we cannot know all other choices that have been and are being made about scarce resources by people around the world. This is the way God designed us, for only he is all-knowing. Our sin compounds our ability to acquire the knowledge we need to accomplish and produce the things we want. Even before the Fall, Adam and Eve faced the knowledge problem because they were finite. They weren't God. Imagine that Eve wanted to make a pie. She would still have to discover how to make it. She would have to learn that wheat can be processed into flour and sugar can be extracted from cane. Before the Fall, with infinite time horizons, this discovery could happen at her pace and without her starving. After the Fall, failure to learn better ways of farming and food manufacturing costs lives. Here we see again the power of economics as a tool for overcoming this challenge.

The economy allows people to trade with one another and achieve greater flourishing, as individuals specialize in their comparative advantage, act in their own self-interest, and make choices based on subjective value. In addition to knowing the actual choices people make and

---

1. Friedrich A. Hayek, "The Use of Knowledge in Society," *American Economic Review* 35, no. 4 (1945): 519–30.

understanding why they make them, prices are another key part of the economy that sends signals to market participants about subjective value.

In a market where individuals have choices, scarce resources can move freely to their highest valued use. This happens when buyers reveal their preferences to sellers. This creates potential profit opporutnities which induce or encourage those potential and existing sellers to fill the most urgent needs of consumers. This rationing mechanism sends important signals that no central planner, or even a very good president, could ever know. Market systems do not require us to find the best and smartest people to run them; they rely on a system of property rights, prices, and profit/loss signals to coordinate dispersed and self-interested strangers.

Prices communicate information that we would otherwise have no way of knowing. As individuals participate in a market using countless resources in countless ways and making decisions based on their local knowledge and subjective value, the movement of prices communicates the breadth of dynamic local information to all market participants. Prices can tell producers and consumers how much resources and services are valued based on their opportunity cost. Consumers can tell producers how much they value items in the market based on how much they are willing to pay. By sending signals about scarcity and subjective value, prices help us cope with the knowledge problem by giving economic actors a way to share exclusive information and make informed choices based on price signals.

The way that prices relay information allows suppliers and consumers to communicate subjective value. The way prices send signals ensures that resources are directed to their highest valued use. One key way they do so is through profit and loss. When consumers value a good or service, they will consume it and the supplier will profit. This informs the producer that the specific use of resources is creating value and they should continue to act on those signals. A producer experiences losses when resources are not being put toward their most valuable end use.

Property rights are a foundation of the way prices communicate information. People who own property have an incentive to care for and improve it, and they only serve to benefit by stewarding what they own.

Prices and property rights are valuable tools for navigating all of the constraints resulting from living in a fallen world. Prices send powerful information about subjective, vast, and otherwise unknowable information. Property rights are a driving factor behind accurate price information. They align incentives to ensure that there is an interest in accurately assigning prices to make the most of scarce resources. Prices and property rights work together to relay information about scarcity and subjective value at every stage of the economy.

ASSIGNMENTS

1. Friedrich August von Hayek, "The Use of Knowledge in Society"
2. Art Lindsley, "Private Property"
3. Walter Kaiser, "Ownership and Property in the Old Testament Economy"
4. Russell Roberts, "Where Do Prices Come From"
5. Donald J. Boudreaux, "Information and Prices"
6. Shawn Ritenour, "Three Reasons Private Property Is Essential for Human Flourishing"

OPTIONAL RESOURCES

- Jeffrey A. Tucker, "Hayek: The Knowledge Problem"
- Morgan Rose, "Information, Prices, and Socialism's Flaws"
- Armen A. Alchian, "Property Rights"
- PovertyCure, "Private Property Rights" (must be purchased separately)

STUDY QUESTIONS

In a few sentences, answer each of the questions below after completing the assigned reading.

1. What does a free-market economy mean? Which institutions are involved in a free-market economy? What is the outcome?
2. How do prices emerge in the free market?
3. Explain what it means to say that prices serve as a resource allocation tool.
4. What kind of information do prices communicate to the buyers and sellers in a market?
5. How do prices help overcome the decentralized nature of knowledge?
6. If prices are emergent and based on scarcity, how will we ever know if a price is "too high"?
7. What is the function of profits? Of losses? What would happen if we didn't have profits and losses?
8. What incentivizes companies and individuals to supply their goods and services in the marketplace?
9. Why is it important that prices are flexible?
10. What would happen to incentives without private property? What would happen to productivity? Why?
11. What inspires and results from profit and loss?

GROUP OR FAMILY ACTIVITY

Consider the prices of fruit, nuts, meat, dairy products, ice cream, and water on your next trip to the grocery store. Take notes about what information could be wrapped up in those prices and how many people were involved in making decisions to make these products available on the shelves.

SUMMARY

Trade is instrumental in bringing about higher levels of flourishing. Prices are integral to directing the most efficient and effective trades. In order to secure all of the related incentives, property rights give economic agents a stake in creating value. Ownership is an incentive to create value, and, therefore, to accurately reflect all associated information in the form of prices.

We are unable to know all things about all resources at all times. We can only completely understand our own subjective value, not that of others. Yet we are still faced with making choices. Ownership of property and the prices that the ownership informs help us to make those choices. As prices pass through so many levels of the economy, they evolve to reflect nearly complete information.

Next week we will talk about how subjective value plays into our knowledge constraints. In the coming weeks we see how profit-seeking (manifestation of self-interest) helps economize on knowledge and serve others.

MODULE 6

THE MARKET PROCESS, SUBJECTIVE VALUE, AND UNPLANNED ORDER

DESCRIPTION

The market is a process through which individuals come together to trade with each other. This trade is driven by self-interest. This self-interest is guided by subjective value, and in pursuit of always improving our conditions. Voluntary trade benefits both parties. We will never know how much any person gains from an individual trade because subjective value is so deeply embedded in who we are as people. We often can't articulate it, and it can change from day to day. We can assume that if we are not being forced to trade, we are gaining from the trades we make. But a trade we are willing to make today we may not make tomorrow.

LEARNING OBJECTIVES

- Understand the importance of market trade for overcoming the knowledge problem and allowing people to trade based on their own subjective values.

- Because no one has everything they need, trade provides the opportunity for one stranger to get what he or she needs by figuring out what other strangers need and want and providing it for them.

- We all value things differently. This is part of who God made us to be.

KEY IDEAS

1. It is necessary that we be able to trade freely because we each value things uniquely and according to our own preferences. One person's idea of how much a particular item or service is worth can be very different from that of another. Thus, the ability to engage in mutual and voluntary exchange results in the mutual benefit of all parties involved.

2. Markets and trade lead to flourishing because they account for dynamic individual preferences and subjective value. They are the best way to allocate scarce resources to their most highly valued uses, satisfying individual preferences and mutually benefitting all

29

participants in free-market exchanges. It is the way we cultivate creation as we are told to do in Genesis. Market trade allows distinct and unique individuals, each with their own God-given purpose, to serve others based on trade through relative comparative advantages.

3. Trade will only occur if Person A values Person B's goods or services enough to exchange resources for them. This gives Person A motivation to create something that Person B will find valuable and worth trading for. Trade generates the prospect of gaining benefit by producing something valuable, thus encouraging that production.

INTRODUCTION

In a previous module we discussed the important distinction between self-interest and greed. Self-interest is an important part of our creation. We are intentional, rational, and purposeful agents. We seek to improve our current state of affairs, which is why we do things like brush our teeth and eat our vegetables. These things may not be inherently pleasurable in the way that going swimming or playing soccer is pleasurable, but we do them because we know they are good for us. Seeking and accepting the sovereignty of Christ is also in our self-interest, but it's not always easy to deny our selfish ways and go where God leads us. In this regard, pursuing our self-interest, that which is good for us, is not always fun—but it is always good. Greed is always sinful and starts as a heart posture of idolatry that hurts others when acted upon.

The pursuit of self-interest is how God created us to act as purposeful creatures. Self-interest drives our choices, and economics is all about choice: what incentivizes it, what discourages it, and why. Our unique, subjective evaluations of the things we do and do not value drive our self-interest. Some like the color green more than the color blue. This in itself is not an economic choice but a personal preference. When we purchase things that are green, we make an economic choice based on our subjective value. Have you ever stood in front of your kitchen pantry and deliberated over what to eat for an afternoon snack? Your family probably stocks the pantry with similar items from week to week, so you usually have a good idea of what is available. Even so, you can't decide what you want to eat at any given moment. This is part of your subjective value. It can be based on your mood, what you ate recently, how tired you are, what commercial you just watched, and many other things.

Because people value many different things, the market process has a reason to provide products for consumers according to those desires. Take a stroll down the peanut butter aisle the next time you go to the grocery store. There are probably at least fifteen types of peanut butter: smooth, creamy, crunchy, natural, etc. There are also many different peanut butter alternatives or substitutes because some people are allergic to peanuts or perhaps just prefer other nuts. This gives consumers many choices, including alternatives like almond or sunflower butter. Suppliers have an incentive to provide these choices to consumers because consumers have different tastes and preferences. This applies to peanut butter, cars, computers, and smart phones. Consumers drive what producers and suppliers make because the suppliers can only make a profit when they satisfy the subjective values of consumers. The market process, through the emergence of prices, brings the most willing suppliers together with the most willing customers, creating many choices for people. When this happens with a great deal of competition, with many firms competing to sell us peanut butter and cars, for instance, we are better off because firms compete on both price and quality. As a result, items become better and relatively cheaper over time.

This process helps us fulfill the goal of flourishing as presented in Genesis. The market helps us to cultivate the earth, take dominion, and to bring about more flourishing than there otherwise would be. We are all talented at different things, and when people can specialize in their gifts, it frees the rest of us who are not good at those things to do what we are good at doing. Purchasing a car frees you from having to figure out how to make one on your own, something most of us could never do. When you can purchase from fifteen or more types of peanut butter, you don't have to grow peanuts, something most of us don't know how to do either. When people can focus on cultivating their talents and trade through markets, firms are directed to always seek ways to create value.

The market encourages the service of others and, on net, encourages investment and personal sacrifice. This said, sin is always with us and often distorts our subjective value. Sin separates us from God. It distorts not only what we want but the time in which we want to consume it. Sin may drive us to want sinful things, things we should never partake in, or it might make us covet things that aren't inherently sinful. The fact that we each have our own unique subjective values is not sinful, but what we value and why we value it can be sinful. If we go into debt to obtain based on covetousness, then we are likely engaging in idolatry. This does not imply that all debt is bad, but it can be if we are putting the things our debt gets us above Christ. The smartphone isn't sinful itself, but our pursuit of it could be. This is why we must constantly surrender to the sovereignty of Christ and be in constant prayer about the desires of our hearts.

ASSIGNMENTS

1. Max Borders, "Subjective Value"
2. Brian Baugus, "How Does the Market Work?"
3. Russell Roberts, "The Reality of Markets"
4. Anne Bradley, "The Market Process and the Path to Flourishing"
5. Russell Roberts, "A Marvel of Cooperation: How Order Emerges without a Conscious Planner"
6. Friedrich August von Hayek, "Kinds of Order in Society"

7. Anne Bradley, "Is the Economy a Pie?"

8. Hans Rosling, "200 Countries, 200 Years, 4 Minutes" (video)

9. Tom W. Bell, "Can Order Be Unplanned?" (video)

10. Donald. J. Boudreaux, "Subjective Value" (video)

11. Steven Horwitz, "Spontaneous Order and the Market Process" (video)

OPTIONAL RESOURCES

•   Daniel B. Klein, "Rinkonomics: A Window on Spontaneous Order"

•   Donald J. Boudreaux, "Individual Flourishing and Spontaneous Order" (Chapter 3 of *The Essential Hayek*)

•   Aeon J. Skoble, "Subjective vs. Objective Value: The Economist and the Philosopher" (video)

STUDY QUESTIONS

In a few sentences, answer each of the questions below after completing the assigned reading.

1. Can biblical flourishing and economic progress coexist? Why or why not?

2. How does a market economy ration goods? What is the role of market trade in resource allocation?

3. How does the free-market system incentivize people and companies to supply goods and services to others?

4. How can we apply what we know about human anthropology to how people make decisions in the market? Are human anthropology and the function of the market compatible? If so, explain how. If not, explain the incongruities.

5. How is it possible to create value if we are bound by scarcity?

6. Explain spontaneous order. How does it emerge in the market?

7. Discuss free trade and coercion in terms of whether they can ensure mutual benefit, and why or why not.

8. Imagine you have two autographed baseballs that you want to sell online. When people bid, the Derek Jeter baseball reaches $1,140, but the baseball signed by your little league coach only reaches $14.50, including the bucket of baseballs that comes with it. What explains the difference in prices?

GROUP OR FAMILY ACTIVITY

Take the family to the grocery store and let your children have fifteen minutes to browse the store. Ask them to make a list of their ten favorite items in the store, and jot those ten items on an index card. Share the lists with each other when you get back home. Did anyone have the same favorite items on their lists? Why or why not? What made an item number one versus number ten? Do you think that could change on your own personal list?

SUMMARY

The market is a constant, ongoing process driven by the subjective valuations of consumers to whom firms and sellers respond. We get greater material flourishing when the market process is butressed by good governance and the rule of law. The lives of all are better, especially the lives of the poor. The market process is decentralized and sophisticated. No one person can drive it or manage it. God created us differently so that we can serve each other with our gifts and talents, whether you are a software engineer, an accountant, or a small-business owner.

The market process unleashes human creativity, generating entrepreneurial discovery and allowing us to make more from less. It helps us fulfill our role as subcreators in God's kingdom. Only God can create something out of nothing, but we can and are called to create something out of something and the market process facilitates that over time.

MODULE 7

PRICES, PROPERTY RIGHTS, AND PROFITS

DESCRIPTION

Economist Peter Boettke often refers to the necessary "three P's" in economics: prices, property rights, and profits and losses.[1] Those three P's gives us the "three I's": incentives, information, and innovation. We need property rights to incentivize individuals to produce and make investments with their human and financial capital. Prices emerge through individual trade based on property rights and the ability to make contracts. These prices give individuals the information they need to assess how much they want a certain good or service based on their subjective values. Profits and losses give important information to suppliers and entrepreneurs about how well they are satisfying consumer wants and needs.

At its core, economics is about making good decisions that glorify God. This week we will learn about the importance of prices and profits for good decisions.

LEARNING OBJECTIVES

- Understand that profits are what we should seek in all situations, whether it is profit in time or money. Profit is what is left over after we have made any investment. Profit encourages the prudent use of resources and filling the needs of others.

- Understand that without prices we cannot understand the underlying levels of scarcity in a society. When the price of lumber changes we can know something about whether it became more scarce (price increase) or less scarce (price decrease).

- For prices to signal information that we could not otherwise acquire we must allow them to be nimble. Government price controls limit the free movement of prices and therefore the free movement of resources.

---

1. "Boettke on Mises." Hosted by Russell Roberts. EconTalk. *Library of Economics and Liberty*, December 27, 2010, www.econtalk.org/archives/2010/12/boettke_on_mise.html.

KEY IDEAS

1. Applications of supply/demand

   a. The demand curve represents the relationship between price and the desire to consume that particular good—it is a negative or inverse relationship. As the price decreases, buyers will purchase more goods and services.

   b. The supply curve represents the positive relationship between the price offered and the amount a seller is willing to bring to the market. As the price increases, sellers will bring more goods and services for sale.

   c. When the supply curve and demand curve intersect we can understand our "equilibrium price and quantity," meaning the market process has brought together the most willing sellers and buyers.

   d. External factors can shift both the supply curve and the demand curve. You should understand what shifts those curves and the new market equilibriums.

INTRODUCTION

Last week we learned about how the market works: it is a process. Markets are dynamic and always in motion. They are driven by purposeful human beings who seek to better their current conditions, motivated by their unique and God-given subjective values. This week we will see how the three P's—prices, property rights, and profits—help us to better trade and increase overall societal wealth. To do that we will use some basic economic modeling to help us understand how supply and demand work and how prices are formed.

As we look at different scenarios, we will see how interactions in the market result in what economists call "equilibrium prices." This is the temporary intersection of the supply and demand curves. These are not fixed points in time; they are always moving and changing based on consumers' desires, constraints, and the relative changing nature of scarcity. As an extension of the scenarios, we will see how prices are critical in solving the knowledge problem and understand why prices cannot be set arbitrarily. Ultimately, this application will continue to solidify the idea that economic freedom leads to the most human flourishing.

As we learn more about the market, we will continue to see how all levels of the economy are integrated. In the exercises of this module, we will learn what drives supply and demand curves. We should remember prices are sending signals at all levels of the market. If the price of bread goes up, something is likely happening to the price of bread's ingredients. Prices reflect that change. Only people who value bread at the higher price will continue to buy it; others will switch to a substitute. If bread producers see fit, they will be incentivized to innovate and find a way to lower prices and regain consumers. If prices are high because of a shortage, high prices will stay high to communicate scarcity, ensuring bread lasts people through the shortage.

By the same token, prices cannot be artificially set. Price ceilings and price floors, set by someone regardless of market interactions, illustrate the potency of the knowledge problem. When these types of prices are set, humanity experiences deadweight loss—resources do not go to their highest valued use because prices cannot move freely to communicate what that use is. As a result, peoples' choices are diminished.

Prices are an inalienable part of trading with one another. We even see prices at work in the Bible, allocating scarce resources when there is a siege or famine. Prices give us a common language to communicate value so we can reach higher levels of flourishing through more trade. Freely moving prices allow us to fully cultivate the creation set before us and not let value go to waste. This is our task as subcreators.

ASSIGNMENTS

1. David R. Henderson, "Demand"
2. Robert Sirico, "Why Profits are Not Exploitative"
3. Armen A. Alchien, "Property Rights"
4. Robert Sirico, "Prices Keep Profits Fair"
5. Anne Bradley, "Making a Profit: An Unexpected Way to Help Others"
6. Michael Munger, "Can Price-Gouging Laws Prohibit Scarcity?"
7. Alex Tabarrok, "The Demand Curve" (video)
8. Alex Tabarrok, "The Supply Curve" (video)
9. Alex Tabarrok, "The Equilibrium Price" (video)
10. Tyler Cowen, "A Deeper Look at the Demand Curve" (video)
11. Tyler Cowen, "The Demand Curve Shifts" (video)
12. Alex Tabarrok, "A Deeper Look at the Supply Curve" (video)
13. Alex Tabarrok, "The Supply Curve Shifts" (video)
14. Alex Tabarrok, "Exploring Equilibrium" (video)

OPTIONAL RESOURCES

1. Alex Tabarrok, "Does the Equilibrium Model Work?" (video)
2. Alex Tabarrok, "Supply and Demand Terminology" (video)

STUDY QUESTIONS

In a few sentences, answer each of the questions below after completing the assigned reading.

1. What are some factors that can shift the supply curve?

2. More graphing of supply and demand:

   a. Graph the effects of an increase in income on the market for pizza.

   b. Graph an increase in the demand for peanut butter on the market for jelly.

   c. A drought hits Idaho, graph the supply response in the market for potatoes.

   d. How does supply respond when we levy a tax on gasoline used for cars? How would the supply or demand curve would shift on a graph?

3. What happens when something or someone who is not a market participant, such as a law or a central planner, artificially sets prices?

4. Why would it cost $25 to park in downtown DC but only $2.50 to park in Houston, Texas? What do these disparities reflect? Are parking lot owners greedier in DC and more altruistic in Texas? Are there better-quality parking spots in DC?

5. If a country is faced with a bad wheat crop, would they run out of wheat? Why or why not?

6. Evaluate the validity of the following statement: When milk prices rise, it is because supply decreases and demand increases.

GROUP OR FAMILY ACTIVITY

1. Watch "Does the Equilibrium Model Work?" (under optional readings). Have everyone gather five items to sell in your store. Collect information from your family on what they are willing to pay and construct the demand curve. Based on the price at which you are willing to sell an item, construct a supply curve. What is the equilibrium price for each of your goods?

2. Choose five household items. What factors would cause the demand curve to shift for these items? What factors would cause the supply curve to shift?

SUMMARY

This week, we took a closer look at the mechanics of supply and demand. Understanding the way these curves interact with each other, reflect peoples' choices, and communicate information allows us to appreciate the role of prices in directing resources to their most highly valued uses.

Prices are key to us being the most productive subcreators possible, for they represent information that is important to making wise economic decisions, and thus, stewarding creation. We saw this in the exercises of shifting supply and shifting demand curves: prices reflect what is going on throughout the economy. Looking at supply and demand curves allows us to appreciate the role economic freedom plays in flourishing. The examples of price floors and price ceilings show that prices must move freely to help us avoid wasting our scarce resources.

Economic freedom allows resources to find their equilibrium price as a result of innovation, scarcity, and peoples' needs and demands. Overall, freely moving prices incentivize getting the most out of our scarce resources. The resulting competition drives prices down, allowing human flourishing to spread.

MODULE 8

ECONOMIC FREEDOM AND STEWARDSHIP

DESCRIPTION

We need freedom to obey the cultural mandate and put our God-given creativity and talents to work. If God is calling you to open a small business, you need to be unencumbered by regulations and corruption to do that. The *Economic Freedom of the World 2015 Annual Report* is a way to measure the material flourishing that is possible in a society.[1] When people live in a society with economic freedom we can say that they live in an opportunity society in which they are freer to pursue what God calls them to do.

LEARNING OBJECTIVES

- Understand the five pillars of economic freedom.
- Understand the outcomes of economic freedom.
- Understand the consequences when human beings don't live under economic freedom.

KEY IDEAS

1. The importance of freedom for economic progress.
2. The level of economic freedom represents the level of individual opportunity.

INTRODUCTION

We've previously learned that the market process helps allocate scarce resources, and scarcity is the biggest constraint we must constantly work to overcome, whether it is scarcity of our time, talent, resources, or money. The market helps humans cooperate with one another and work

---

1. James Gwartney, Robert Lawson, and Joshua Hall, *Economic Freedom of the World 2015 Annual Report*, with the assistance of Ryan Murphy, Hans Pitlik, Dulce M. Redín, and Martin Rode (Fraser Institute), http://www.freetheworld.com/2015/economic-freedom-of-the-world-2015.pdf.

together with strangers to produce more for less. For this to work we need conditions of economic freedom to be present, which allow individuals to work, earn incomes, start businesses, and create value for others.

There are five pillars of economic freedom:

- The size of government is small relative to the size of the economy
- Rule of law
- Freedom to trade
- Sound money
- Levels of regulation

When these five pillars work together, individuals have greater opportunities to cooperate and serve one another. The market process is a story of the coordination and cooperation of anonymous strangers. When we think of it this way, it seems miraculous that we can find thousands of items waiting for us in a Walmart, and at lower prices over time. For this to happen we must have economic freedom, broadly described as a society rich with opportunities.

A society with economic freedom has a government that is limited and focuses on the protection and defense of the property rights of individuals. Government that is limited is restrained to protect the freedom of individuals and foster an environment where people can live into their gifts and serve each other. It is a society in which each of us are free to wake up each morning and pursue our vocations, whether as an artist, a mom, a janitor, or a CEO. We need to pursue these roles with integrity and excellence if God has called us to them. A society rich with economic freedom ensures that we have the opportunities to do these things. Economic freedom does not guarantee we will be rich or never have sorrow or suffering. Flourishing can and will include trials, sacrifice, and some suffering because we live in a fallen world marred by sin.

Scripture tells us that trials are part of our journey. James 1:1–4 tells us to "consider it pure joy, my brothers and sisters whenever you face trials of many kinds, because you know that the testing of your faith produces perseverance. Let perseverance finish its work so that you may be mature and complete, not lacking anything." Economic freedom will not eliminate trials, but it will allow us to bring about biblical flourishing better than we otherwise could.

Consider a woman who lives in the Democratic Republic of the Congo. This country ranks near the bottom of the *Economic Freedom of the World 2015 Annual Report* at 144 out of 157 countries.[1] On a scale of 0–10 (zero being no economic freedom and ten being perfect economic freedom), it scores a 5.65. This score reflects the miserable conditions that men, women, and children must

---

1. Ibid.

fight every day. Each and every day she must focus on getting drinking water for her family by traveling many miles and gathering dirty water from a river used by animals. She must then carry it back to her village. This activity requires a great deal of calories. The water that she drinks is something we in the first world would not consider drinking. She does it because it is crucial for her survival, but it takes up many of her productive, waking hours each day.

Being saddled with this day in and day out means she does not have time to pursue her other, potentially more valuable gifts and talents. The world is worse off for this. If she was a citizen who experienced economic freedom, she could get clean water fortified the way you do. She would be free to pursue other things. Increasing levels of economic freedom saves lives and benefits the world because it allows people to focus on cultivating their gifts and talents, rather than being saddled with activities that are difficult and time-consuming.

ASSIGNMENTS

1. James D. Gwartney, Richard L. Stroup, and Dwight R. Lee, *Common Sense Economics*, Parts 2 and 3
2. Alan S. Blinder, "Free Trade"
3. Anne Bradley and Joseph Connors, "Economic Freedom and the Path to Flourishing"
4. Anne Bradley, "Five Reasons Christians Should Embrace Economic Freedom"
5. Econ Free, "Economic Freedom and Quality of Life" (video)
6. Econ Free, "Economic Freedom in America Today" (video)

OPTIONAL RESOURCES

- Donald J. Boudreax, *The Essential Hayek*, Chapters 4–6
- Antony Davies, "What's So Great about Economic Freedom?" (video)
- Robert A. Lawson, "Economic Freedom of the World" (video)
- Josh Hall, "Economic Freedom and Growth" (video)
- Josh Hall, "Economic Freedom and a Better Life" (video)
- Robert A. Lawson, "Economic Freedom"
- Randall G. Holcombe, "Economic Freedom and Economic Growth: Political Freedom, without Economic Freedom, Does Not Bring Growth"

STUDY QUESTIONS

In a few sentences, answer each of the questions below after completing the assigned reading.

1. Discuss which institutions and rules of the game are driving or inhibiting the success of the top ten and bottom ten countries in terms of economic freedom, respectively.

2. Explain how and why voluntary exchange creates value.

3. Give an example of a policy with an unintended consequence. How would economic thinking have helped prevent it?

4. Discuss the idea of the growing economic pie. Does the government create value? Why or why not?

5. If we are bound by scarcity, why are standards of living so much higher now than they were two hundred years ago, even though the resources at our disposal have not changed?

GROUP OR FAMILY ACTIVITY

Have each family member compare the United States to one country they are passionate about or interested in and compare their Economic Freedom Scores using the "Heritage Foundation 2016 Index of Economic Freedom."

1. Does the United States have more or less economic freedom? Why?

2. Does the comparison country seem to be getting more or less economic freedom?

3. Of the five pillars of economic freedom, which are lacking or decreasing in your countries?

4. What would it take for the United States to start gaining economic freedom?

SUMMARY

Economic freedom is critical for us to do what God has called us to do: be good stewards of his creation by using our gifts and talents to serve others. When we are saddled with corrupt governments, high levels of monetary inflation, poor property rights, the absence of trading partners (limited trading opportunities), and excessive government regulations, we cannot thrive in the way God desires for us. Economic freedom allows the market process to thrive and fosters the creative spirit with which God endowed us. Economic freedom is something we in the first world often take for granted because it's all we have experienced. It is not something to take for granted. According to the *Economic Freedom of the World 2015 Annual Report*, the United States was number two in the world in economic freedom in 2000 and has been falling ever since.[1] This drop in

---

1. Ibid.

our score is something to be concerned about because it is more difficult for people to use their gifts to serve others, harder to open businesses, and harder to comply with complex regulations. Christians must advocate for economic freedom because of our desire to live out God's commands, especially the cultural mandate, and his desires for his creation.

MODULE 9

ENTREPRENEURSHIP AND INNOVATION

DESCRIPTION

The cultural mandate tells us to work the garden and take care of it. This happens when we make good decisions and use our gifts to cultivate God's creation in an effort to serve others. One important way we serve others is by finding new ways of doing things. This is what entrepreneurs do. They tinker, invent, and innovate. It would be a mistake to think that the only people who do this are entrepreneurs like Bill Gates. Even in the lowliest jobs, we can better the conditions of others by finding better and cheaper ways to do our work. Entrepreneurs drive prosperity by innovating. It is God's design for us that the work of our hands can glorify him, have lasting and eternal significance, benefit us through the paycheck we receive, and fulfill the needs of others.

LEARNING OBJECTIVES

- Understand the role that entrepreneurs play in a free society and what happens when a society does not have good incentives for people to innovate.

- Understand that the role of entrepreneurs is difficult—they have to predict future prices.

KEY IDEAS

1. Competition is good, but perfect competition shouldn't be our goal.
2. Economic freedom is critical for the development of future entrepreneurs.

INTRODUCTION

Last week, we brought together all the concepts we have learned in order to explain economic freedom, which allows us to be the best stewards we can be. Economic freedom enables us to trade with the fewest barriers to serving each other and with incentives to make others better off, directing us to make the most of scarce resources. This week, we will explore the power of

44

competition. We will also learn that in a system of economic freedom, certain pressures direct efficient outcomes. We call these pressures the laws of supply and demand.

When the five pillars of economic freedom work together, there are more opportunities for us to serve one another in the market and thus to bring about more flourishing. As entrepreneurs come to the market to provide more choices to more consumers, we can experience more variety. This allows people to specialize in what they were called to do, because we can all come together and share in what the market has to offer us. The combinations available to satisfy our unique subjective values are vast and many.

As there are more opportunities for suppliers to enter the market, consumers reap the benefits. In a free-market system in which excessive regulations do not limit who can enter and exit a market, more suppliers can pursue their profit-seeking self-interest. The incredible part of this pursuit is that consumers benefit the most. In order for a supplier to succeed in making a profit, they must provide what is being demanded at a price that is consistent with how consumers value it. Consumers will engage with suppliers who provide the best quality for the lowest price. Under economic freedom, everyone's benefit is encouraged because the more competition suppliers face, the more they are incentivized to provide the highest quality product at the lowest price. Thus, prices are perpetually driven down, as the goal is to find more efficient ways to supply. All of humanity benefits from this system, because it ensures that we get the most out of scarce resources and continue to innovate to meet demands and increase quality of life. As the cost of supplying people with things they need and want decreases, more of those resources are required to satisfy our demand. This frees up precious and scarce resources.

Under economic freedom, consumers control the future by purchasing what they demand for prices they find fair. Supply and demand applies to everything traded in the market—goods, services, and all of the inputs for those goods and services. The free market allows the movement of prices based on supply and demand, such that even wages reflect the value of a service being provided. In this module, we will begin to see the application of how prices communicate information and serve as a method for rationing scarce resources.

When there is a high demand for a product or service, relative to other things, there is an incentive to supply. Entrepreneurs are those who have the gift of recognizing this demand and working to meet it. The prices set for goods and services are based upon what consumers are willing to pay. If the cost of production is higher than the price consumers are willing to pay, then producing that product is an inefficient use of resources; the resources should either go to another use, or the producer should determine a more efficient way to supply the product using fewer resources. In the end, innovation occurs to make the most of our scarce resources. Prices speak volumes in the market as they allow consumers and suppliers to find an equilibrium price—a price that makes it worthwhile for the supplier to supply (based on costs of production and profit margin desired, alternatives, etc.) and also makes it worthwhile for the consumer to consume, based on their subjective value.

Economic freedom allows the market process to thrive, which is revolutionary for bringing about human flourishing. When we have economic freedom, people come together to trade in a way that makes the most of our scarce resources and benefits the most people. Prices allow a vast network of suppliers and consumers at all levels of the economy to communicate subjective value based on needs, preferences, and scarcity. Consumers can communicate what they are willing to pay, and suppliers can communicate the minimum price at which they are willing to supply. Prices are instrumental in our calling to bring about flourishing in a world of scarcity. Given the knowledge problem, the movement of prices in a free market is the only way to ensure we cultivate creation in the most rewarding, least wasteful way possible.

In a market where there is freedom to buy and sell, suppliers are incentivized to answer consumer demands. Furthermore, they are incentivized to do so at the highest quality and at the lowest price, so that they can secure profit. Nothing is static; the goal is to constantly improve. As more suppliers enter the market, more choices are provided and more people can benefit, since the goal is to provide what consumers demand.

ASSIGNMENTS

1. Ludwig von Mises, *Profit and Loss*
2. Wolfgang Kasper, "Competition"
3. Brian Baugus, "Entrepreneurship within a Biblical Worldview"
4. Elise Daniel, "Meet the Generation Bringing Back Entrepreneurship in America"

OPTIONAL RESOURCES

• Matthew Mitchell, "Dinosaur Wars: When Competition Goes Extinct" (video)
• Hugh Rockoff, "Price Controls"
• Paul Heyne, "Efficiency"

STUDY QUESTIONS

1. Why is it that competition is a good thing, but perfect competition is not the goal?
2. What does competition encourage?

3. What incentives does a company have in a competitive market? Who benefits from competition?

4. What is the role of the entrepreneur in bringing about more freedom for others? How does this happen?

5. Name three ways one can be an entrepreneur.

GROUP OR FAMILY ACTIVITY

Think of someone your family knows who owns their own business; maybe this is your own family. What did they have to figure out before they could open their business? How did they predict future prices? How does profiting help them to stay in business and help others? What do you think is the most difficult thing they do?

SUMMARY

Economic freedom allows the market process to thrive. It fosters the creative spirits with which God endowed us. It incentivizes innovation and directs the most efficient uses of resources. In a market where there is freedom to create, improve, buy, and sell, suppliers are incentivized to answer consumer demands, and they are incentivized to do so at the highest quality and the lowest price so they can secure a profit. This makes the most of scarce resources and encourages the use of those resources to bring about flourishing.

MODULE 10

MIDTERM

KEY IDEAS

At this point in the course, you should be able to:

1. Describe the components of the economic way of thinking.

2. Expound upon the value of the economic way of thinking, given how God created us.

3. Recognize the tools God has given us to fulfill the cultural mandate and bring about flourishing.

4. Define and explain the relationship between comparative advantage and calling, and the relationship between comparative advantage and trade.

5. Point to examples of work, trade, and stewardship in Genesis and throughout the Bible.

6. Outline the relationship between comparative advantage, scarce resources, and trade-offs.

7. Outline the problems that the free market solves, and how.

8. Recognize how economics is a tool for stewardship.

9. Define and give examples of subjective value and its relationship to trade.

10. Clarify the types of incentives put in place by the free market.

11. Define trade-offs and opportunity cost.

12. Recognize areas of your life in which greater flourishing is made possible through trade.

13. Describe how value is created in a world of scarcity.

14. Exemplify how trade makes us better off than we would be otherwise.

15. Understand how the market directs self-interest.

16. Clarify the need for property rights in order to achieve value creation.

17. Illustrate how prices communicate information.

18. Explain what encourages innovation.

19. Illustrate the drivers of economic progress, even though our resources have always been scarce.

20. Communicate the dynamics of the knowledge problem and how prices help us overcome it.

21. Clarify why competition, profit, and loss are conducive to flourishing.

22. Illustrate how equilibrium prices are met and the importance of freely moving prices.

23. Distinguish factors that would shift a supply and demand curve.

24. Define and explain the importance of economic freedom to flourishing.

25. Communicate how we can overcome scarcity.

26. Recognize instances of a growing economic pie. Explain how a free trade economy is a growing pie and define the key elements that make this flourishing possible.

27. Expound upon the components of a market economy and its results.

28. Explain biblical stewardship in the context of economics.

SUMMARY OF KEY IDEAS

We are subcreators living in a fallen world, tasked with bringing about flourishing and unleashing our creativity to fulfill what God asks of us (his desire) in Genesis: to fill the earth and subdue it.

Scarcity was made worse by the Fall. Due to this, we now live in a world of scarce resources, and none of us have the infinite time or talents to provide for all of our own needs. Furthermore, self-interest is woven into our human design. We have learned there are biblical roots of self-interest and a direct link between self-interest and the way the market economy directs flourishing. Economics helps us to be better stewards. As self-interested individuals, the economy incentivizes value creation, and trade brings us together to make the best of our God-given design. Value creation and greater human flourishing are the result.

In order to bring about flourishing in a world of scarcity, we need to do two things. First, we need to understand how God created us, and second, we need to embrace an economic system that directs choices for the sake of greater flourishing. Ultimately, this means that we need to make decisions consistent with the economic principles that God ordained in the creation of humankind and that result in greater flourishing. God's design is not for us to live in poverty, and economics is one of the tools he has given us to make ourselves and others better off as we make the most of our scarce resources. Based on the way God made us and the way he made the world, the economic way of thinking is a helpful tool for making choices that please him and that he promises will bring about flourishing.

The economic way of thinking involves recognizing the importance of a system that directs peoples' choices in a way that brings about flourishing. This means there has to be a way to communicate the subjective value housed within each of us, incentives to create value, opportunities for people to do what they are good at, and trade with others to enjoy a wider variety of goods and services. Fortunately, we were each made with a calling and a comparative advantage. When we each focus on what we were designed to do and can come together through trade, we can better navigate this world of scarcity. Since we cannot provide everything we need for ourselves, economic freedom allows us to enjoy far greater levels of flourishing. We are able to focus on what we do well, and trade with others to accumulate the rest of what we need.

We are better off having a system that brings us together to trade, which frees us from having to labor to provide for all of our needs. Instead of laboring to provide for all our needs, we can focus on the things that we are relatively better at doing, do those things well, and then come together to trade with each other.

Trade and comparative advantage are a powerful combination. We realize we were not created to do all things well, but trade allows us to conquer some of our scarcity by fostering specialization and the division of labor. We see in Scripture that we are uniquely made in God's image to use our creativity to advance flourishing of his creation and glimpse the way things could and will be when they are restored.

Trading not only allows us to enjoy more by expanding our possibilities and increasing our quality of life, it also incentivizes value creation, which brings about flourishing. Value creation is inextricably linked to bringing about flourishing in this world of scarcity. As voluntary and mutually beneficial exchanges compound, we are working toward flourishing.

When there is freedom to trade, everyone is able to improve their lot based on their subjective value. Value is increased because people can continue trading to improve their well-being. That's the goal of trading: value creation. Property rights and the potential to profit incentivize good stewardship of our scarce resources because there is competition to provide the highest quality product at the lowest price.

Flexible prices are key to trading goods and services, for they accurately communicate value about scarcity, supply and demand, and subjective value.

In this scarce and finite world, all choices involve costs and trade-offs. The Fall made fulfilling God's design and desires much more difficult; therefore, we succumb to sin daily. As a result, it is harder and flourishing is often untenable. In a world of sin, we need a system to help us not only help ourselves, but also to help others find fulfillment and flourishing. It is critical that we understand that all choices involve trade-offs so we can attempt to make the most valuable decisions given the unchangeable factors.

This is how economics helps us become better stewards. We learn to count the costs and look at the possible unintended, unforeseen consequences of our actions. We are better able to navigate an uncertain and unpredictable world. Further, the power of profit and loss incentivizes us to create value by reconciling costs and benefits to ensure that we make the most of our scarce resources and time.

The irreplaceable value of free trade is further communicated when we study the knowledge problem we experience as part of our human condition. We cannot know everything about all time and things. We can only completely understand our own subjective values, not those of others. Yet we are still faced with making choices. Prices are key instruments helping us make those choices. Prices provide us with a common language allowing us to communicate necessary, though not always complete, information. Faced with the knowledge problem, we are fortunate God has given us the market system as a way to communicate knowledge we cannot fully encompass. When property rights secure the incentives to create value and prices are allowed to be flexible, prices move to reflect the status and value of goods and services and direct the most efficient and effective trades.

The market is a constant and ongoing process; it's driven by consumers making subjective valuations and the firms and sellers who respond to them based on their subjective valuations. When the rule of law, to which even political officials must submit, is in place, we can achieve greater material flourishing, because people can choose how to serve one another based on subjective value. Because trades are mutually beneficial, everyone's life becomes better when they trade over time. The knowledge problem means that no one person can drive or manage the market in a way that maximizes value, because every agent has their own subjective value. Rather, God created each of us uniquely, so that we can serve each other with our gifts and talents through the market process, based on localized knowledge and subjective value. With the freedom to engage in mutually beneficial exchanges based on localized knowledge, the exchanges driving the market process unleash human creativity as we work to fulfill our role as subcreators in God's kingdom.

In order to engage in the market process in a way that brings about flourishing, we need certain conditions allowing individuals to work, earn incomes, start businesses, and create value as entrepreneurs for one another. Economic freedom is critical for us to be good stewards of God's creation by using our gifts and talents to serve others. It consists of five pillars: the size of government being small relative to the size of the economy; rule of law; freedom to trade; sound money; and levels of regulation. When these five pillars work together, individuals have more opportunities to cooperate to serve one another and are encouraged to create value and fulfill the call to creativity.

In addition to learning the inextricable links between the market processes and flourishing, you also learned the mechanics of the economy: supply and demand. By understanding the way these graphs move, we see how prices solve the knowledge problem, why prices cannot be artificially set, and how the market encourages innovation. With economic freedom, goods and services can find their equilibrium price, which is a product of consumer demands and supplier competition driving prices down while bringing quality to the market.

SHORT ANSWER QUESTIONS (PARENT/TEACHER CHOOSE NO MORE THAN TEN QUESTIONS FOR THE STUDENT TO ANSWER)

1. When do we see trade take place in Genesis? Are we created to serve each other through our gifts?

2. What does it mean to think like an economist?

3. What is a free-market economy? Which institutions are involved in a free-market economy? What is the outcome of trade?

4. Does anyone know how to make a pencil? Why does this matter?

5. What about our human anthropology makes interdependence and trading important? Can we flourish alone? Why can't we divide up all resources equally?

6. How and why does division of labor make sense biblically and economically? What are the advantages of division of labor for the individual and for society?

7. How can we think of biblical stewardship within the context of economics?

8. Why do we need incentives to make decisions? Can't we just rely on altruism?

9. What can we tell about demand from the supply curve? Why?

10. Can suppliers sell their goods and services at any price they want? Explain.

11. Will technology ever eliminate scarcity? How does our call to creativity help reduce scarcity and increase options?

12. What are some things that can shift the supply curve?

13. Delineate the importance of prices, trade, and resource allocation. How are prices set in the free market?

14. If prices are emergent and based on scarcity, how will we ever know if a price is "too high"?

15. What is the function of profits? Of losses? What would happen if we didn't have them?

16. How can we think about biblical flourishing and economic progress? Can those things coexist?

17. What is the role of market trade in resource allocation? How does the free market incentivize people to supply goods and services to each other?

18. Explain the difference between greed and self-interest. Is it unbiblical to act out of self-interest? What is the role of self-interest in market trade?

19. What happens when prices are artificially set by something or someone who is not a market participant, such as a law or some central planner? Why is this the result?

20. If scarcity necessitates a rationing mechanism, why is competition beneficial?

21. How does demand for high-tech cell phones in the United States encourage cell phone use in third-world countries?

22. See the chart below. For each "market" draw a supply and demand curve and label the equilibrium price and quantity. Then graph what happens to that original market after the stated event and mark the new equilibrium. Discuss the results and how they impact our lives. How is each different?

Market	Event
Gasoline	Hurricane Katrina
Lemons	Frost destroys half the nation's crops
Margarine	There is a decrease in the price of butter
Peanut butter	Increase in the price of all jellies
Cars	Decrease in the price of subway rides

23. What is the policy implication of voluntary trade among strangers being a positive sum?

MODULE 11

ECONOMIC FREEDOM AND THE DEVELOPING WORLD

DESCRIPTION

Christians have a mandate to care for the poor. Jesus ministered and cared for those who were poor, orphaned, widowed, and vulnerable. We must do the same, but good intentions are not enough. We must be good decision makers, considering both the costs and the consequences of our choices when we seek help for the poor. The best long-term and sustainable solution to poverty is to elevate the dignity of the person by enabling them to use their God-given creativity to serve others. This requires economic freedom, which will provide greater opportunities for the poor.

LEARNING OBJECTIVES

- Markets help the poor by providing greater access to goods and services.

- Things that we might consider the toys of the rich, like smartphones, are powerful tools that could provide the poor with greater opportunities.

- There are long-term societal benefits of allowing the poor to unleash their creative talents in the world.

KEY IDEAS

1. The role that the far reach of the market plays in making everyone better off.
2. Comparative advantage and the spread of wealth and access to goods and services.

INTRODUCTION

As subcreators, human beings have a job to do on Earth as described in the cultural mandate given in Genesis: "And God blessed them. And God said to them, 'Be fruitful and multiply and fill the earth and subdue it, and have dominion over the fish of the sea and over the birds of the heavens and over every living thing that moves on the earth'" (Gen. 1:28). We are to subdue the natural world, take dominion, and use our creativity to bring about flourishing. We are also to exercise dominion of the social world by having families and building communities, churches, cities, and cultures. Nancy Pearcey puts it this way in her book, *Total Truth:*

> Redemption is not just about being saved *from* the consequences of sin, it is also about being saved *to* something – to resume the task for which we were originally created. And what was that task? In Genesis, God gives what we might call the first job description: "Be fruitful and multiply, and fill the earth and subdue it." "Be fruitful and multiply", means to develop the social world: build families, churches, cities, governments, laws. The second phrase, "subdue the earth" means to harness the natural world: plant crops, build bridges, design computers, compose music. This passage is sometimes called the "cultural mandate" because it tells us that our original purpose was to create cultures and build civilizations—nothing less.[1]

Seen in this light, scripture shows us how everything we do, from reading Shakespeare to composing music, is incredibly profound. If God created us to do these things, either in our work or in our free time, it brings glory to him and to his creation. When we unleash our skills and creativity, we serve others and relieve them of having to accomplish everything on their own. This is a truly liberating biblical and economic insight. Comparative advantage helps us understand what it is we do relatively better than others. When we can rely on others to do things for us that we aren't so good at doing, we are then able to serve each other based on our gifts through voluntary trade.

The expansion of global voluntary trade that spread through much (but not all) of the world at the onset of the industrial revolution profoundly changed specialization and the division of labor, two concepts Adam Smith emphasizes as necessary for wealth creation. Recall that the first part of Smith's *An Inquiry into the Nature and Causes of the Wealth of Nations* explains that the increasing division of labor frees us from being specialists in everything and allows us to specialize in what we are good at doing.[2]

This fosters the growth of market exchange.

---

1. Nancy Pearcy, *Total Truth: Liberating Christianity from Its Cultural Captivity* (Wheaton, IL: Crossway, 2008).
2. Adam Smith, *An Inquiry into the Nature and Causes of the Wealth of Nations* (London: Methuen & Co., 1904).

The developing world currently lacks access to market exchange, which would free the poor from having to rely on themselves for everything they need. We have a more difficult time flourishing when we are in these circumstances. The woman who has to collect dirty water from the local river and purify it in a crude manner will never have the same quality water that comes through our kitchen tap. We don't have to think about water, which frees us to think about and create other things. The woman in Africa is trapped; the acquisition of water takes most of her productive and caloric energy every day, and she has little left over for creative work and education. This is the plight of the poor in the developing world. An industrial revolution would help with unleashing of comparative advantages, trade, and access to goods and services that we need and want to survive.

According to the World Bank, there has never been more hope that we can eliminate abject poverty than there is today.[1]

As Christians, we must take this seriously if we are to play a positive role in the process. Economics helps us understand that while our mission trips are important for sharing the gospel and satisfying the need for food, medical care, and shelter in the short term, they cannot jump-start economic growth. Our poverty alleviation efforts must consider what long-term economic progress looks like for the poor and ask how we can facilitate their economic growth by fostering trade with them.

ASSIGNMENTS

1. Sara Corbett, "Can the Cell Phone Help End Global Poverty?"
2. Laurence Chandy and Geoffrey Gertz, "With Little Notice, Globalization Reduced Poverty"
3. Robert E. Lucas Jr., "The Industrial Revolution: Past and Present"
4. Derek Thompson, "The Economic History of the Last 2,000 Years: Part II"
5. Tolu Ogunlesi and Stephanie Busari, "Seven Ways Mobile Phones Have Changed Lives in Africa"
6. The World Bank, "Mobile Phone Access Reaches Three Quarters of the Planet's Population"
7. Hans Rosling, "200 Countries, 200 Years, 4 Minutes" (video)
8. Hans Rosling, "Hans Rosling and the Magic Washing Machine" (video)
9. Donald J. Boudreaux, "The Hockey Stick of Human Prosperity" (video)

---

1. Zorobabel Bicaba, Zuzana Brixiova, and Mthule Ncube, "Can Dreams Come True? Eliminating Extreme Poverty in Africa by 2030," *IZA Discussion Paper Series* No. 8120 (April 2014), http://www.worldbank.org/content/dam/Worldbank/Feature%20Story/Africa//afr-zorbabel-bicaba.pdf/

OPTIONAL RESOURCE

1. Tyler Cowen, "The Malthusian Argument" (video)

STUDY QUESTIONS

In a few sentences, answer each of the questions below after completing the assigned reading.

1. What changed around 1700 to cause the hockey stick of economic growth?
2. How does demand for high-tech cell phones in the US encourage cell phone use in third world countries?
3. Explain how the Industrial Revolution has been a process of global coordination and service.
4. What made the Industrial Revolution different in terms of the spread of global trade?
5. What are the biggest threats to economic freedom in the United States today? What can Christians do to affect this in the future?
6. Consider a country like Pakistan, one of the most destitute places on the planet. What would it take to get greater levels of economic freedom, private property rights, rule of law, and generally good institutions there?

GROUP OR FAMILY ACTIVITY

Interview a missionary family in your local church and document what country they spent time in their ministry. Then examine where this country stands in terms of economic conditions (using the *Economic Freedom of the World Index*). What are the trends in this country based on both the interview and your research? What needs to change for people to be able to trade more effectively? If your family could go on a mission trip, where would you go and how would your economic perspective change what you would want to accomplish?

SUMMARY

Economics helps us understand how to better steward our own talents and serve others. This makes everyone better off. The poor need greater access to goods and services that will help ease their lives and lower their transactions costs. We take products like ice-makers, refrigerators, and washing machines for granted, but they dramatically affect our daily lives by freeing us to play musical instruments, compose poetry, and engage in other activities and hobbies we love. We want this for the poor as well. Economics helps us understand that there are effective and ineffective ways to do this. The next few modules will give us a biblical and economic perspective on how to reduce poverty and bring about greater flourishing for the world as a whole.

MODULE 12

THE ROOTS OF POVERTY

DESCRIPTION

Poverty is a result of the fall of humankind into sin; God did not create humankind in a condition of poverty. It is not part of God's original design, nor is it his desire for us or his creation. In some cases, poverty is caused by our own sin, like the person who becomes addicted to drugs and loses their home. In other cases, it is caused by things not of a person's doing, such as sickness, natural disasters, or outside oppression. Spiritual poverty will always be with us. Material poverty doesn't have to be. Economics can help us bring about greater flourishing through God-honoring decision making.

LEARNING OBJECTIVES

- It is neither virtuous to be poor nor villainous to be rich if we are honoring God in our daily decisions. We can be both rich and righteous.

- Poverty can be overcome as we make better decisions and help others to live into their gifts.

KEY IDEAS

1. Biblical perspectives on the poor.

2. The distinctions between spiritual and material poverty.

3. When things are available for purchase, they are easier to access than if we have to produce them entirely on our own.

4. Economic freedom is the world's best solution to poverty.

INTRODUCTION

If free trade, through the institutions of economic freedom, is able to bring about flourishing, why do so many people still face poverty? In this module, we will explore the roots of poverty in order to help us understand why it exists and the best way to deal with it. Understanding the roots of poverty and the best way to care for the poor is an invaluable application of all that we have learned, especially since the Bible calls us to care for the poor. The Bible is laced with examples of Jesus helping the poor, and we are undoubtedly tasked with doing the same. This module may challenge some typical or conventional approaches to poverty alleviation in order to comprehensively explain how to best care for the poor.

In order to understand how we can best help the poor, we must understand the roots of poverty. Material poverty is not the problem but a symptom of something deeper. Poverty has many causes. It can, for example, be the result of laziness, moral foolishness, death, disasters, or oppression. Poverty will always be with us as we work toward restoration; it is one of the challenges we face as subcreators in a fallen world. Our broken relationships hinder pure human flourishing. Fortunately, we have the tools for bringing about flourishing, and with an understanding of the roots of poverty we can better help those trapped in it. We can embrace and encourage the best environment for poverty alleviation with a clear understanding of the tools we have to bring about flourishing and make the most out of creation.

We can work to care for those who are experiencing poverty, spread the good news of the gospel, and understand how to best use the tools God has given us to bring about flourishing. There is no secret formula to poverty alleviation, but it is key that when caring for the poor we have an understanding of the causes of poverty so that we can provide relief appropriately. We must work to provide relief, rehabilitation, or a longer-term strategy of development, depending on the kind of poverty being experienced. For example, if a village has just experienced a typhoon and is left starving, sick, and in ruins, the first step may be to provide food, shelter, and medical care. Over time, though, the strategy should shift to rebuilding a self-sustaining village that can keep itself out of poverty, so that it is not reliant on handouts. The evaluation and strategy-development is not simple, but the Bible is clear that we must walk with the poor in whatever form they need and help them be who God made them to be.

Understanding what the Bible has to teach us about poverty, paired with understanding economics as a tool to bring about flourishing, can be very powerful in helping the poor. Based on the lessons in this module, we will be able to think critically about responsibilities when it comes to caring for the poor in an impactful way. In some cases, efforts to help the poor can make them worse off: resources can be inefficiently used, their confidence and self-worth damaged, or a cycle of dependency may emerge. Throughout this module, we will consider approaches that will help to alleviate poverty without hurting those in need.

ASSIGNMENTS

1. Jonathan Pennington, "'Sell Your Possessions and Give to the Poor': A Theological Reflection on Jesus' Teaching Regarding Personal Wealth and Charity"
2. Theology of Work Project, "God's Law Calls People of Means to Provide Economic Opportunities for the Poor"
3. Glenn Sunshine, "Who are the Rich and the Poor?"
4. Art Lindsley, "Five Myths about Jubilee"
5. Theology of Work Project, "Productive Opportunities for the Poor"

OPTIONAL RESOURCE

1. Values & Capitalism, "A Jubilee from Good Intentions"

STUDY QUESTIONS

In a few sentences, answer each of the questions below after completing the assigned reading.

1. What does the life of Jesus teach us about wealth and charity?
2. What does it mean to say that we should want to "help the poor help themselves"?
3. What is the gospel solution to poverty? Give an example of how this solution worked in the Bible.
4. List two responsibilities of the church toward the poor, two responsibilities of the rich toward the poor, and two responsibilities of the poor.
5. List the five myths of Jubilee.

GROUP OR FAMILY ACTIVITY

Consider an instance when your family tried to help someone who may have been materially poor, such as handing a few dollars to a homeless person, preparing Thanksgiving dinners, or writing a check to a church's long-term mission efforts. Based on the lesson of this module, how could these efforts have been more impactful?

SUMMARY

Based on the lessons in this module, we can reconsider the responsibilities of the church toward the poor, of the rich toward the poor, and the responsibilities of the poor themselves. We can also begin to gain a deeper understanding of the role of the economy in bringing about flourishing and doing the most lasting good for the most people, which we will explore further in the next module.

Next week we will specifically exhibit the power of the free market in bringing about the most good to the most people. With poverty alleviation as a focal point, we will continue to see how free-market capitalism has, more than any other system, lifted the most people out of poverty and improved well-being en masse. While poverty will always be with us and is a complex challenge, the capitalist economy has proven to be the most successful poverty alleviation program because it creates an environment that has brought the most lasting good for the most people.

MODULE 13

THE ROLE OF ECONOMIC FREEDOM IN ALLEVIATING POVERTY

DESCRIPTION

The market is an emergent process that brings people together based on their subjective values that drive human choice. The most vulnerable around the world are those that are largely exempt from the benefits that markets bring. Thus, poverty alleviation must concern itself not just with giving resources to the poor, but helping the poor to cultivate their creative gifts.

LEARNING OBJECTIVES

- Understand that markets bring greater justice by increasing access to necessary and vital goods and services to all income groups.
- Material well-being frees our time to do other, more productive things to which God calls us.

KEY IDEAS

1. Explain the power of the market to encourage justice and morality, and fight poverty.
2. Relationships with the people we are trying to help is a key biblical and economic insight to fighting poverty.

INTRODUCTION

Last week we considered the responsibilities Christians have to avoid harming the poor while trying to help them. In this module, we will pair that nuanced understanding of poverty with the understanding of how the capitalist economy brings about flourishing.

Free trade has proven to be the most successful poverty alleviation program.[1] The free-market economy creates an environment in which people can continue to trade and increase value. The market process creates incentives for people to make the most of scarce resources by providing the highest quality goods and services for the lowest price. More goods and services are reaching more people around the world as the free market continues to inspire innovation. In addition to the increasing availability, creativity, and utility of goods and services, the prices for these things are decreasing. This decrease results from suppliers aiming to meet the consumer's priority of maximizing value. As more suppliers compete against one another, the supply of goods and services increases, so suppliers focus on lowering prices as much as possible. More people enjoy a higher quality of life as quantities increase and prices decrease.

In addition to encouraging the creation of more goods and services, free-market capitalism provides opportunities for advancing one's future. Creating more value engages more people. For example, as a car company expands its production, it engages employees at all levels of the production process, giving people opportunities to earn income. Globally, everyone becomes better off as these kinds of opportunities compound. A virtuous cycle of opportunity begins as companies provide opportunities for earning income, leading to people increasing their well-being.

Markets do more than improve flourishing by providing better options to market participants. They provide more options to an increasing number of people, too. This module exemplifies how the market continuously provides opportunities for improved quality of life through goods and services that are available, and through opportunities to earn an income.

ASSIGNMENTS

1. Kristine Zambito, "When It Comes to Alleviating Poverty, Here's How Your Church Can Avoid Help that Hurts"

2. Steven Horwitz, "Contemporary Economic Myths"

3. Elise Daniel, "Economic Freedom is Not Enough for Human Flourishing"

4. Robert A. Lawson, "Economic Freedom"

5. Anne Bradley, "Freedom and Flourishing"

6. Jeff Dorfman, "Free Markets Unquestionably Help the Poor"

7. IFWE, "Flourishing" (video)

---

1. Robert Lucas Jr., *The Industrial Revolution: Past and Future 2003 Annual Report Essay* (Minneapolis, MN: Federal Reserve Bank of Minneapolis, 2003), https://www.mineapolisfed.org/publications/the-region/the-industrial-revolution-past-and-future/

OPTIONAL RESOURCES

1. Wesley Gant, "3D Printing Will Break the Malthusian Box—Again"
2. Ronald Demos Lee, "Population"

STUDY QUESTIONS

In a few sentences, answer each of the questions below after completing the assigned reading.

1. Is the market a force against poverty? Why or why not?
2. By discussing their definition and their impact, explain how wealth redistribution and wealth creation are different. What are the implications of each for societal flourishing?
3. Explain how progressive cheapening happens and what effects result from it.
4. How can the church get involved in poverty alleviation? List practical applications from this chapter on programs churches can implement to truly help the poor.
5. For the poor, what are the tangible benefits of increased access to markets?

GROUP OR FAMILY ACTIVITY

How does buying food at a restaurant help a group of people? Who benefitted when the family purchased a family vehicle?

Think back to the lessons on competition, an inherent element of free-market capitalism. How does competition, between companies seeking to secure profit, help improve the lives of poor people? Consider the number of people who owned a cell phone twenty years ago compared to now. How does competition between firms improve the lives of increasing numbers of people over time?

SUMMARY

The free market is the most effective resource allocation system when it comes to alleviating poverty. As we learned in this module, history shows us that free-market systems improve quality of life immensely.

The free market encourages justice and morality, and ultimately fights poverty. In the next module, we will develop a deeper understanding of conclusions drawn in this module by considering counterexamples.

MODULE 14

GOVERNMENT AND THE ECONOMY

DESCRIPTION

The government is an institution that, when operating well, can support the rule of law and protect both people and property rights. These protections provide a robust environment for economic progress, human creativity, and greater economic freedom. Government can also be an entity that takes property, violates human life, and engages in theft. Cronyism is a danger to good government—over time government can be subject to special interests and create winners and losers.

LEARNING OBJECTIVES

- Understand the benefits of government when it is limited and the dangers of government when it goes beyond its proper scope.

- Government always has a cost so when we consider a new policy we must assess the expected benefits, the costs, and the potential unintended consequences.

KEY IDEAS

1. The government, when limited, can be a force for good by protecting property and providing security. Government also has costs, and when able to exceed its limited powers, can be a force for excessive regulations and a decrease in prosperity.

2. Government actors respond to personal incentives which is often why we see government officials seeking extra powers. Because of this, governments succumb to the desires of special interest groups which creates winners and losers (some win and many pay the price). However, the government is not as powerful as free trade in terms of helping the poor escape poverty.

INTRODUCTION

In the last two modules, we took a deeper look at caring for the poor, a challenge that will always be with us. We must understand the best way to care for the poor in order to truly empower them and improve their situations. Then, we need to make connections between the free market's ability to bring about flourishing and the importance of embracing the free market to improve the well-being of the most people over time.

We are called to care for the poor, which is why it is imperative we take a critical look at different approaches to poverty alleviation and their effects. In this way, we will become keenly aware of which approaches work the best, and which ones don't. When it comes to caring for the poor, government provision of goods and services is the main alternative to the free market as a vehicle for flourishing. Exploring this alternative further underscores our understanding of the free market's ability to inspire the innovation and mutual benefit that helps the least among us.

History shows that free-market systems vastly improve quality of life. The way market incentives inspire innovation to make the most of scarce resources leads to competition that improves quality and lowers prices for consumers. Over time, as more and more goods are produced, progressive cheapening allows more individuals to enjoy a higher quality of life. Since we are all unique, some people will always be relatively poorer or relatively richer than others. What is important to remember is that the poor are becoming relatively better off over time.

The government has been assuming more and more responsibility for providing for the poor. This module looks at the common perception of government's role in society and considers whether it is an optimal arrangement for everyone involved.

We will continue to parse out the best way to care about the poor in light of how God created us. Given peoples' subjective values, the knowledge problem, and our existence in the world of scarcity, our economic system and role of government have strong implications for flourishing.

This module also compares the effects of the welfare state on the poor and society as a whole, with an emphasis on what the Bible says about character and caring for the poor. It also takes a historical look at the success of voluntary associations compared to government poverty-reduction programs.

Planning how other people allocate their goods and services cannot unleash flourishing. Because of this, the way the government attempts to aid the poor falls short in many respects, leading to negative results. The practice is inefficient and often misguided, allocating resources in a way that neither the giver nor the recipient of the resources would have chosen given their subjective values. By elaborating on the counterexample of caring for the poor—government aid—this module solidifies the idea that only the pressures of a free market can direct the most efficient outcomes, given how God created us.

We will also emphasize the importance of a free market for creating opportunities for the poor. In an environment where people can come together to trade based on comparative advantage, the poor can benefit by finding some form of employment and from the progressive cheapening resulting from innovation and the supply of more goods and services.

ASSIGNMENTS

1. J. P. Moreland, "A Biblical Case for Limited Government"
2. Robert Murphy, "The Costs of Government"
3. Don Boudreaux, "Free Trade and Globalization: More than Just 'Stuff'"
4. Robert Higgs, "Government Growth"
5. James Madison, "Federalist #10"

OPTIONAL READINGS

1. Thomas MaCurdy and Jeffry M. Jones "Welfare"
2. Learn Liberty, "Working More to Earn Less | Why the Poor Stay Poor" (video)
3. Michael Hendrix, "Helping Actually Can Hurt, New Study Finds"
4. Robert Sirico, "The U.S. after the Welfare State"
5. Robert Sirico, "Is Welfare Compassionate?"
6. Robert Sirico, "Samaritan's Dilemma"
7. Doug Bandow, "Generous with Someone Else's Money"
8. Jim Powell, "Alexis de Tocqueville: How People Gain Liberty and Lose It"
9. Library of Economics and Liberty, "Real vs. Nominal"
10. Lawrence H. White, "Inflation"
11. Michael J. Boskin, "Consumer Price Index"
12. Wesley Gant, "3D Printing Will Break the Malthusian Box—Again"

STUDY QUESTIONS

In a few sentences, answer each of the questions below after completing the assigned reading.

1. Explain how wealth redistribution and wealth creation differ by discussing their definitions and their impact. What are the implications of each for societal flourishing?

2. Does the government provision of goods/services work to the short-term or long-term advantage of the poor?

3. What are the effects of government welfare? Why?

4. What is the biblical role of the state?

5. How does government spending distort the economy, and what effect does it have on private individuals and their decision-making abilities?

GROUP OR FAMILY ACTIVITY

Let's replay the trading game that we played earlier. This time, appoint someone as the central planner and allow them to reallocate the goods with each trade. Compare the amount of value created, the amount of frustration that resulted, and why the outcome was different than in the game of free trade. Why did this occur? How might this occur when the government tries to provide for the poor?

SUMMARY

We have drawn the distinction between planning versus freedom and choices in order to explain why there are certain systems that do and do not lead to flourishing, given the way God created us.

Specifically, we compared the effects of the welfare state on the poor, and on society as a whole, versus the impact of the free market and voluntary poverty-reduction associations.

Since planning for others' allocations of goods and services cannot unleash flourishing, especially when the exchanges between parties are not by choice, the way the government attempts to aid the poor falls short in many respects. We can appreciate the importance of a free market in bringing about opportunities for the poor. Next week, we will look at the unintended consequences of government involvement in the economy and what effect that has on individuals.

MODULE 15

GOVERNMENT AND UNINTENDED CONSEQUENCES

DESCRIPTION

Our actions have immediate consequences. They can also have long-term, unintended consequences. We must consider both if we are to make God-honoring decisions. Government actions can actually hurt those they purport to help. This may not be done intentionally, but when we fail to consider the long-term effects of our actions, we don't envision some of these consequences that can come about.

LEARNING OBJECTIVES

- Learn how to see an action through to its long-term end.
- All our actions bring costs and tradeoffs but some are not initially observable.

KEY IDEA

1. Applied topics: Government and unintended consequences (taxes, minimum wage, transfers, subsidies, price controls, welfare, etc.).

INTRODUCTION

In the last few modules, we have looked at challenges Christians wrestle with, such as poverty. Each of those modules pointed to the free market and the economic way of thinking as powerful mechanisms for overcoming these challenges. The modules also highlighted the harm resulting from unintended consequences of government action. Now we will take a clear look at why government cannot be tasked with bringing about flourishing, and what happens when it alters the market's movements.

Government is not fully equipped to make decisions about how we should allocate scarce resources. Government leaders suffer from the knowledge problem just like the rest of us. You might not know the best ingredients for producing yogurt, the best wage to pay a talented mechanic, or the best quality and price of supplies needed to build certain types of computers. In the same way, government often doesn't know who has the knowledge and incentive to make the most of the resources it seeks to control through rules and regulations. In attempting to help one group, government can hurt another group by changing the flow of the market, where all information is comprehensive and relative to other supplies and demands for other resources. No one is able to know everyone else's preferences, subjective values, or the knowledge needed to solve all resource allocation challenges.

Government also lacks the incentives to make decisions about how we achieve efficiency. These incentives are warped because some elected officials are competing for votes to secure success and profit. When government is in charge of allocating resources, sometimes its actions can be inconsistent with what truly, sustainably maximizes scarce resources. Government leaders may promise short-term fixes to deeply rooted problems. They may take action that creates deadweight loss that would not have occurred if prices could move freely and communicate information.

Since government leaders make decisions based on maximizing votes instead of resources, some goods and services lose their ability to move relative to all other goods and services. Incomplete or false information signals now alter the movement of goods and services based on supply and demand. As this false information is injected into the market via government actions like mandated prices, subsidies, regulations, or quotas, all other decisions are made relative to the new information. Soon, the market is experiencing a slippery slope of unintended consequences.

All decisions in the market directly or indirectly influence other decisions in the market, especially trade-offs and the variables that move supply and demand curves. There are a number of ripple effects when the government alters the movement of goods and services. These ripple effects are what economists call unintended consequences.

In this module, we will look at the unintended consequences resulting from government direction of people, goods, and services toward certain outcomes, for reasons different from those motivating a market participant to maximize value. For example, when government places taxes or subsidies on resources, the cost of those resources as inputs changes, affecting the cost of the product they go into, and inaccurately reflecting the true value of those resources.

Unintended consequences run all the way through an economy. Consider government attempts to fix income inequality. When the government tries to redistribute income from the wealthy to the less wealthy, the restructuring of the economy that occurs does not stop with redistribution. The effects can be quite far-reaching. Say the government takes wealth from upper economic classes via taxes and moves it to lower economic classes via welfare and tax refunds. This redistribution discourages members of both the upper and lower economic class to earn income. Taking profit earned by value creation dampens the incentive to continue creating value. This harms the entire economy. In a free-market economy, profit is a sign of creating value, and creating value means that more peoples' lives are improved over time.

Regardless of the government's motives, there are unintended consequences to their actions. This is especially dangerous when the party creating the consequence is not part of the economy.

ASSIGNMENTS

1. Frédéric Bastiat, *The Law*
2. Frédéric Bastiat, *What Is Seen and What Is Not Seen*
3. Anne Bradley, "Does the Minimum Wage Hurt the People It's Trying to Help?"
4. Lord Brian Griffiths, "Christianity, Socialism, and Wealth Creation"
5. Antony Davies, "Unintended Consequences of Price Controls" (video)
6. Alex Tabarrok, "Price Ceilings" (video)
7. Alex Tabarrok, "Price Ceilings: Rent Controls" (video)
8. Alex Tabarrok, "Price Floors: The Minimum Wage" (video)
9. Alex Tabarrok, "Price Floors: Airline Fares" (video)

OPTIONAL RESOURCES

1. Henry Hazlitt, *Economics in One Lesson*
2. Thomas J. Dilorenzo, "Hurricanes Are Creative Destruction?"
3. Robert P. Murphy, "5 Unintended Consequences of Regulation and Government Meddling"
4. Burton Folsom, "The Origin of American Farm Subsidies"
5. Steve Horwitz, "The Importance of Failure"
6. George Reisman, "Price Controls and Shortages"
7. Dwight R. Lee, "The Perversity of Doing Good at Others' Expense"
8. *The Freeman*, "The Truth about the Minimum Wage" (video)
9. Learn Liberty, "The Broken Window Fallacy" (video)
10. Learn Liberty, "Does the Minimum Wage Hurt Workers?" (video)

11. Rob Norton, "Unintended Consequences"
12. Daniel A. Sumner, "Agricultural Subsidy Programs"
13. Linda Gorman, "Minimum Wages"
14. Marginal Revolution University, "Commodity Taxes" (video)
15. Wesley Gant, "Minimum Wages Make Jobs Worse"

STUDY QUESTIONS

1. Is it possible for the government to ration goods based on needs? Why or why not?

2. Are government subsidies given to farmers because certain crops are so expensive to grow, or are certain crops so expensive to grow because the government offers price supports?

3. What is the triple hypothesis according to Bastiat?

4. How does the law get misused as a tool for empowering special interests?

5. Discuss the unintended consequences of the minimum wage in light of the true effects of redistribution we studied last week. How is this different from the free-market outcome?

6. Why can't we just wait for the government to provide goods and services? Where does the government get its resources?

GROUP OR FAMILY ACTIVITY

Watch "Does the Minimum Wage Hurt Workers?" by Learn Liberty and discuss the following:

- What are the unintended consequences of raising the minimum wage? Who does the policy hurt and who does it help?

- What perverse incentives might motivate politicians to promise to raise the minimum wage?

- How would employers change their decision-making process if the minimum wage increases? Think about Al, Bob, and Carl from the video.

- How does the minimum wage affect minimum wage workers and employers?

- How does changing the minimum wage affect non–minimum wage earners?

- What would the low-wage market look like if there were no minimum wage? Would more people be better off? How and why (or why not)?

- Who has the best knowledge to set wages for employees?

SUMMARY

In this module, we learned why government officials cannot make decisions about the economy and the dangers of doing so. Not only are they unequipped to make such decisions because of the knowledge problem, but they can also be motivated by perverse incentives. Government intervention in the economy is dangerous, since its actions, regardless of motive, will have unintended consequences.

As a result, we should understand why the government cannot be tasked with bringing about flourishing, and the depth and breadth of results that occur when it alters the market's movements.

If we understand the knowledge problem, we can recognize why government cannot establish rules and regulations impeding the free flow of resources to the people with the right knowledge and incentives to make the most of those resources. In attempting to help one group, government can hurt another group by changing the flow of the market, where all information is comprehensive and relative to other resources. Only God is all-knowing enough to know just how to bring about flourishing. Otherwise, it is impossible for any central group or individual leader to have the knowledge needed to solve all resource allocation challenges.

Government also lacks the incentives to make decisions about how we achieve efficiency. Incentives are warped because elected officials are competing for votes in order to secure success and profit. Government may be establishing certain economic rules and regulations with short-term motives, endangering our path to flourishing. This module elaborated on the dangers of an unlimited government by discussing examples of unintended consequences running all the way through an economy.

MODULE 16

FINAL REFLECTIONS

In this final module, we encourage a reflection on the whole course and the specific results discerned in the previous module.

COURSE SUMMARY

This course is about learning the importance of the economic way of thinking as it pertains to our Christian calling to bring about greater flourishing through good stewardship. Stewardship requires us to figure out what we do best and to specialize in that. Economics requires that we embrace realities that we wish did not exist. There is a cost to everything we do because time is our most precious and scarce resource. We must use our time, talents, and resources to further God's kingdom in the most effective way possible. Scarcity, costs, and unintended consequences are economic realities affecting us in much the same way the reality of gravity affects us. If we act without regard to these realities, we do so at our peril.

As you finish the course we hope you are encouraged to know that one of the best ways you can personally contribute to flourishing is to specialize in what you do well. This is why economists focus on division of labor and comparative advantage. Division of labor frees us from having to do all things well. We can focus on our comparative advantage, serving others with *our* gifts. We are able to trade for things we don't do so well, allowing others to serve us with *their* gifts. This is why voluntary market trade is so important. It brings us together and encourages the service of others, rather than the plunder of others.

Trade is also important for global wealth creation and long-term flourishing of the poor. Helping the poor escape poverty requires us to answer the biblical call to exercise dominion over the earth, working it and stewarding it as God commanded in Genesis. We have the privilege of doing that in our own unique ways. God's creation best glorifies him when it functions as he intended. When we do our work well, we reflect the image of God, who is a master creator and artist. Sin makes this more difficult, but our original calling has not changed. We need the economic way of thinking to help us make the most significant contribution we can possibly make.

The economic way of thinking helps us recognize that Pakistan is one of the most destitute places on the planet not because its people are less ambitious or less intelligent. It is because they do not live within the productive institutions of economic freedom which foster the creation of value.

Places without economic, political, and religious freedom foster the plunder of others and tend to be ruled by tyrants. Government plays an important role in protecting our God-given person, property, and purposes. This is because of our human nature. With anything human there is always a potential for greed, plunder, and theft—even within the confines of what appears to be a limited and legitimate government. We must be vigilant around these ideas and demand that our governments respect and protect our freedoms.

As you wrap up the course, we encourage you to think about how these economic realities affect your life personally and how, by embracing them, you can personally contribute to societal flourishing. Economics does not allow us to perfectly predict the future, but it does and should give us a healthy dose of humility as we consider what we can and cannot do, both personally and with policy.

KEY IDEAS

Here are eight key concepts you should understand as you finish the course:

1. We face constant trade-offs because our choices impose costs.
2. We are called to be good stewards and to fulfill God's design and desire for us. We must count all transaction costs to do this well.
3. Self-interest drives our choices. While damaged by sin, it can still help us flourish.
4. We are better positioned to trade with others when we focus on developing our talents.
5. Voluntary trade is a win-win for all, and frees our time.
6. People can best pursue what God wants them to do and serve others when societies have high levels of economic freedom.
7. Government plays an important role in protecting our rights and freedoms. When government does this, it fosters trade and entrepreneurship.
8. Biblical flourishing is our goal, and the economic way of thinking helps us to achieve it.

ASSIGNMENTS

1. Peter Boettke, *The Battle of Ideas: Economics and the Struggle for a Better World*
2. Art Lindsley, "The Biblical View of Freedom"
3. EconStories, "'Fear the Boom and Bust' a Hayek vs. Keynes Rap Anthem"

ASSESSMENT

Write a one-page reflection paper about the three biggest insights you learned from economics and how they will change the way you look at the world.

MODULE 17

FINAL EXAM

MULTIPLE CHOICE QUESTIONS

1. Which of the following is true?

    a. Scarcity and poverty are the same thing.

    b. Poverty means that some basic need of a person is not being met.

    c. Scarcity is the result of price gouging.

    d. All of the above are true.

2. Economics is the study of

    a. How to become a good entrepreneur.

    b. How to make money in the stock market.

    c. How the morals and values of people are formed.

    d. How individuals make choices under conditions of scarcity.

3. Which of the following is consistent with the basic economic postulate that incentives matter?

    a. Consumers buy fewer cars when the price of cars rises.

    b. Farmers produce less corn when corn prices decline.

    c. A politician votes for a subsidy when it is in the best interest of a special interest group within his district even if it might harm other voters.

    d. All of the above.

4. The highest valued alternative that has to be given up in order to choose an action is called

    a. Scarcity

    b. Absolute value

    c. Opportunity cost

    d. Sunk cost

5. Which of the following is not scarce?

    a. Time

    b. Money

    c. Pencils

    d. Air

    e. None of the above

6. The law of comparative advantage suggests that

    a. Individuals, nations, and states can all benefit if they trade with others.

    b. Free trade among nations harms economies.

    c. Every person and economy should strive to be self-sufficient.

    d. Each person should try to produce as much at home as they can.

7. Private property rights exist when property rights are

    a. Transferrable to others

    b. Protected legally

    c. Exclusively controlled by the owners

    d. All of the above

8. Which of the following would allow the production-possibilities frontier for an economy to shift outward?

    a. Better institutions and governance, like converting from socialism to a market-based society.

    b. An increase in the labor force or resources.

    c. More investment which results in better technology.

    d. All of the above

    e. None of the above

9. The owners of private property will

    a. Use their property for selfish ends, taking no account of the impact their behavior has on others.

    b. Use their property in ways that others value because the market will generally reward them for it.

    c. Engage in poor environmental stewardship.

    d. Lose profits when they take the wishes of others into consideration.

10. When Benjamin Franklin wrote "Remember that Time is Money!" he understood

    a. that property rights create incentives.

    b. the law of comparative advantage.

    c. biblical stewardship.

    d. the concept of opportunity cost.

TRUE/FALSE

Students please write a two- to three-sentence explanation for your answer:

1. In each trade, there is a winner and a loser. Voluntary trade cannot make both parties better off.

2. Property that is privately owned tends to be better cared for and better preserved than property that is not privately owned.

3. Consumers will purchase fewer hamburgers at higher prices than at lower prices if other factors remain the same.

4. An increase in the demand for coffee would cause its price to rise and producers to expand output.

5. The law of supply reflects the willingness of producers to expand output in response to an increase in the price of a product.

ESSAY QUESTIONS (CHOOSE SIX)

These should take three to four paragraphs to answer:

1. Discuss how our own call to work in Genesis necessitates that we use the economic way of thinking when we make decisions.

2. Discuss how the article "I, Pencil" demonstrates that market economies bring us into community with one another.

3. Talk about how the Hayek reading "The Use of Knowledge in Society" relates to the reading "I, Pencil."

4. What do prices do in a market setting? Discuss specifically how they operate as signaling devices.

5. List the five components of economic freedom. Which is most in jeopardy in the United States today and why?

6. What does doing our jobs well, as God has called us to, have to do with helping the poor?

7. Why does market trade result in higher levels of prosperity?

8. What is the most important lesson you have learned about economics in this class, and how will it change your outlook in the future?

GRAPH SHIFTING

1. In the market for motorcycles, what happens when the wages of motorcycle workers decrease?

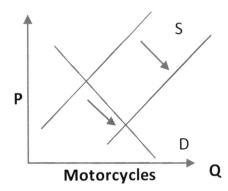

2. In the market for lemons, what happens when a frost destroys half of the lemons in Florida?

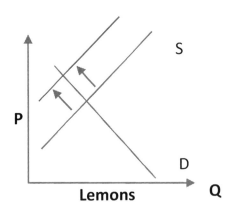

3. If peanut butter and jelly are complimentary goods, what happens to the jelly market when peanut butter becomes cheaper?

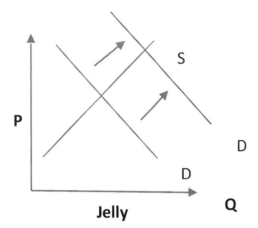

4. In the market for smartphones, what happens if there is a decrease in economic freedom and everyone's incomes decline?

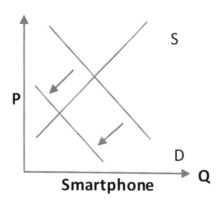

5. If Blu-ray players become cheaper, what happens in the market for DVD players?

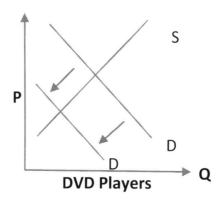

Price	Initial Quantity Demanded	Quantity Supplied	New Quantity Demanded
$2	60	20	80
$4	50	30	70
$6	40	40	60
$8	30	50	50
$10	20	60	40

6. See the chart above and graph the following:

   a. The initial demand curve

   b. The initial supply curve

   c. The equilibrium price

   d. The area experiences economic progress and everyone wants more. See the "New Quantity Demanded" column and graph it.

   e. What is the new equilibrium price?

   f. Has demand changed or is this a change in quantity demanded?

BIBLIOGRAPHY

Bicaba, Zorobabel, Zuzana Brixiova, and Mthule Ncube. "Can Dreams Come True? Eliminating Extreme Poverty in Africa by 2030." *IZA Discussion Paper Series*, no. 8120 (April 2014). http://www.worldbank.org/content/dam/Worldbank/Feature%20Story/Africa/afr-zorobabel-bicaba.pdf.

Boettke, Pete. "Boettke on Mises." By Russ Roberts. *EconTalk*, audio podcast, December 27, 2010. www.econtalk.org/archives/2010/12/boettke_on_mise.html.

Gwartney, James, Robert Lawson, and Joshua Hall. *Economic Freedom of the World 2015 Annual Report.* With the assistance of Ryan Murphy, Hans Pitlik, Dulce M. Redín, and Martin Rode. Vancouver, BC: Fraser Institute, 2015. http://www.freetheworld.com/2015/economic-freedom-of-the-world-2015.pdf.

Hayek, Friedrich A. "The Use of Knowledge in Society." *American Economic Review* 35, no. 4 (1945): 519–30.

Lucas, Robert, Jr. *The Industrial Revolution: Past and Future 2003 Annual Report Essay.* Minneapolis, MN: Federal Reserve Bank of Minneapolis, 2003. https://www.minneapolisfed.org/publications/the-region/the-industrial-revolution-past-and-future.

Pearcy, Nancy. *Total Truth: Liberating Christianity from Its Cultural Captivity.* Wheaton, IL: Crossway, 2008.

Pennington, Jonathan. "A Biblical Theology of Human Flourishing." McLean, VA: Institute for Faith, Work & Economics, 2015. http://tifwe.org/resource/a-biblical-theology-of-human-flourishing-2/.

Ritenour, Shawn. "An Unexpected Source of Human Flourishing." Institute for Faith, Work & Economics blog, March 11, 2015, https://tifwe.org/an-unexpected-source-of-human-flourishing/.

Smith, Adam. *An Inquiry into the Nature and Causes of the Wealth of Nations.* London: Methuen & Co., 1904.

START HERE

The Institute for Faith, Work & Economics provides many resources to help you live a life of freedom, fulfillment, and flourishing. These tools are designed to fit into your life and provide biblical encouragement and guidance to your walk with God.

RESEARCH

Download free in-depth studies to further your understanding of faith, work, and economics.

RESEARCH.TIFWE.ORG

BLOG

Get our daily or weekly blog updates in your inbox.

BLOG.TIFWE.ORG

SOCIALIZE

Connect with IFWE on social media and join the conversation.

FACEBOOK.COM / FAITHWORKECON
TWITTER.COM / FAITHWORKECON

BOOKSTORE

Get our latest releases and
educational products.

STORE.TIFWE.ORG

DONATE

Become a partner in bringing
about flourishing.

DONATE.TIFWE.ORG

PARTICIPATE

Find information about
student groups, upcoming
events, and other
opportunities to get involved.

CONNECT.TIFWE.ORG

11699397R00060

Made in the USA
Middletown, DE
15 November 2018